# GUIDE TO MBA PROGRAMS IN CANADA

# Guide to MBA Programs in Canada

Catherine Purcell

**ECW PRESS**

**1 9 9 1**

CANADIAN CATALOGUING IN PUBLICATION DATA

Purcell, Catherine
    Guide to MBA schools in Canada

ISBN 1-55022-131-0

1. Business education – Canada – Directories.
2. Master of business administration degree –
Canada – Directories.   I. Title.

MF1131.P87 1991 650´.071´171 C91-095008-3

Design and imaging by ECW Type & Art, Oakville, Ontario.
Printed and bound by Hignell Printing Limited, Winnipeg, Manitoba.
Distributed by Butterworths Canada, 75 Clegg Road, Markham, Ontario L6G 1A1.

Published by ECW PRESS, 307 Coxwell Avenue, Toronto, Ontario M4L 3B5

# CONTENTS

*Appendixes:*

# ACKNOWLEDGEMENTS

I would like to thank all the students who so willingly talked to someone they had never met and gave an hour of their time talking about their experiences. I appreciate their honest and open conversations. I would also like to thank the administrators for taking the time to be interviewed and supplying me with the statistics on their schools.

From a personal standpoint, I would like to thank the people who encouraged me and believed in me — my husband Michael; my colleagues David Cannon and Jim Kelly; my good friends Michele Lawson and Elaine Bradley; my parents; and Professor Akenson who acted as a sounding board and information source.

# *Introduction*

The purpose of this book is to help people considering an MBA to differentiate between schools and to answer common questions regarding the MBA degree. The MBA programs are not ranked. The emphasis is placed on what is unique about each one and where the programs' strengths and weaknesses lie. Comparisons among schools are made in the "Comparative Statistics on Canadian MBA Programs" chapter, and special characteristics are highlighted in the "Unique Characteristics" chapter.

The administration and approximately ten per cent of the student body from each school were interviewed to gain a balanced perspective. A selection of at least two of the student interviews that I conducted are included in each university's chapter.

The administration was asked:

- to fill out a questionnaire on the statistical profile of their school, their part-time program, and how they dealt with placement
- what they felt was unique about their program
- what myths they had encountered when talking to applicants
- what kind of student they were looking for.

The students were asked:

- why they chose the school they were attending
- what they felt the program's strengths were
- where the program could improve
- if they were supported in their job search
- what it was like to live in the city as a student
- if they felt the MBA had helped them.

I decided on these questions on the basis of my conversations with thousands of students during my past five years as a career counsellor.

## ABOUT THE STUDENTS INTERVIEWED

An effort was made to select students to represent the points of view of both men and women, full-time and part-time students, and people who had full-time work experience and those who did not. The majority of the students interviewed were in the second year or near the end of their MBA. It was felt that these students would have a better overview of the program than a first-year student. To remain as objective as possible, students who held office in the student government were usually not included.

Five to ten per cent of the full-time student body were interviewed. Trends were looked for when identifying outstanding professors. Most of the students were selected by the school's administration in accordance with the above mentioned criteria. Some students were selected by the referral of a fellow student.

The descriptions of the cities where the MBA programs are based, are a composite of the perceptions held by the students interviewed.

## ABOUT THE STATISTICS

The statistics for each school are for the class of 1990–91. The statistical profile of each school includes information ranging from the academic requirements of the program to other related programs offered by that university. If a category does not appear, it is because the information was not available. Requirements and the deadline dates for admission to part-time programs are the same as for the full-time program unless otherwise noted.

Be advised that the schools do not use a standard method of collecting data. For example, some schools may calculate the average grade point average (GPA), Graduate Management Association Test (GMAT), or the average age of the students in their program based on the applicants that were offered admission, others on the basis of those that were accepted, or other variations. The statistics are to be used only as a guide.

# Ten Myths Surrounding the MBA

The following myths are a summary of comments made by people directly involved in making decisions on admission.

## 1. THE MBA IS A TICKET TO A GOOD JOB AND A HIGH SALARY

During the 1970s when so few people had an MBA degree, there may have been some merit to this statement. Twenty years later, the increasing number of people with MBA's, combined with the decreasing number of middle-management positions, has swung the law of supply and demand in favour of the employer. Today, employers are looking for the best qualified MBA. The emphasis is on the person instead of the piece of paper.

The MBA degree attempts to develop and enhance critical thinking and analytical skills. It changes a person's focus from one area within an organization to the organization as a whole.

Graduating with an MBA will prove that you have the stamina, determination, and the ability to learn, but it is up to the individual to prove themselves. Without a prior record of significant achievements, an MBA will probably not change a candidate's job prospects.

## 2. COMPETENCY IN MATHEMATICS IS NOT REQUIRED

The MBA degree does require an analytical mind-set. The majority of the first year of an MBA program is quantitative, including courses in financial accounting, macro and micro economics, quantitative methods, and statistics. Only basic mathematical concepts are required, but if a person has a phobia about mathematics he/she will have to work much harder.

## 3. AN MBA PUTS YOU ON THE FAST TRACK

There is no such thing any more as a "fast track." Demographics show that the bulge of the population, the "baby boomers," have reached middle management. Corporate down-sizing has made upward mobility difficult, leaving fewer positions available for "baby boomers" and the new graduates behind them.

One strategy some recent MBA graduates have used to bypass the "boomers" is to change organizations several times in the first ten years. Some start with a big corporation to get training and experience. When their advancement is halted, they leave and go to a smaller company where they might be able to get a higher position. Once they have gained the middle- or upper-management experience that they probably would not have had the opportunity to get at the larger organizations, they are able to return to the larger corporation to compete for upper-management positions.

## 4. THE MBA PROGRAM WILL TEACH ME ALL I HAVE TO KNOW

In most cases the MBA is a two-year program. The first year takes people from a wide variety of backgrounds and gives them a basic foundation and a set of analytical tools. In the second year of the program, it is sometimes possible to concentrate in a particular area or continue in a general theme. The program can not possibly prepare future managers for all situations they may encounter. It simply gives them a good background and an overview to solve problems or deal with situations as they arise.

## 5. YOU HAVE TO HAVE A BACHELOR OF COMMERCE/ BUSINESS ADMINISTRATION DEGREE

This is definitely not true. Schools of business are looking for students who have a wide diversity of educational backgrounds to enrich the experience-pool that students can draw on.

Based on 1990–91 class data, the University of Manitoba had the highest per cent (91%) of enrolled students with backgrounds other than business. With 65%, York University had the lowest.

## 6. THE WORK LOAD WILL BE LIKE IT WAS AT THE UNDERGRADUATE LEVEL

The MBA program is purposely designed to be highly demanding in terms of workload. By increasing the workload beyond what one person could accomplish, business schools force students to work together in groups to meet the demand. Developing team building and time management skills prepare students for the work place.

## 7. AN MBA PROGRAM IS FOR MEN

Historically, few women have applied to MBA programs, but their numbers are gradually increasing. The percentage of women enrolled in MBA programs ranges from twenty to fifty per cent with the modal average of thirty-three. Business schools are actively trying to encourage women to apply by offering scholarships to women. Telephone campaigns by current women students are also meant to encourage women applicants.

## 8. IT IS DIFFICULT TO ENTER AN MBA DEGREE PROGRAM WITHOUT WORK EXPERIENCE

Some schools such as University of Calgary, Concordia University, Ecole des Hautes Etudes Commerciales, Queen's University, University of Toronto, University of Western Ontario, and others indicated in the individual school chapters have made a conscious effort to only admit candidates with work experience. Candidates without work experience would have to be academic stars to be seriously considered for these programs. However, other schools such as Université de Moncton, University of Ottawa/ Université d'Ottawa, Simon Fraser University, University of Windsor, York University, and others admit a significant percentage of students immediately following their undergraduate degree.

## 9. SOME EMPLOYERS VIEW MBA GRADUATES AS NOT BEING TEAM PLAYERS

Most Canadian MBA programs are addressing this issue by stressing group work as an integral part of their program. Cases are discussed and prepared in groups, and group projects are typical — all emphasising co-operation and trust.

At first, students often feel that they have to do all the work themselves, and they are reluctant to trust the other members in the group with partial responsibility for their grades. However, the work load is so heavy that they soon realize that they must rely on each other to get the assignments done.

# 10. GOOD WORK EXPERIENCE WILL MAKE UP FOR POOR GRADES

While first-class standing may not be required, work experience cannot entirely compensate for below-average grades. Most business schools are part of the Faculty of Graduate Studies and, therefore, have to meet their minimum academic requirements.

In exceptional cases, certain MBA schools do admit applicants who do not have an undergraduate degree. For a list of these schools and the conditions required, please refer to the chapter "Unique Characteristics."

# Pitfalls of Admission

The number-one reason for being refused admission is because the candidate simply does not meet the minimum requirements. The number-two reason is that the program is not suited to the applicant's expectations. Persons directly involved with the MBA admission process are looking for evidence that an applicant can succeed in the program. Some of the factors that are used to assess candidates are grade point average (GPA), Graduate Management Admission Test (GMAT) score, statements of purpose, résumé presentation, reference letters, and the interview. All of these factors may not apply to each school. Advice on pitfalls specific to one particular school will be mentioned in that school's chapter.

The following advice was compiled from conversations with the administration on the schools' admission committees.

## GPA

Consistency is looked for. If your grades in your core subjects are good but your electives are poor, this might indicate that you do not apply yourself to something you don't like. In the first year of the MBA program, the majority of courses are compulsory, and there may be courses you won't like.

Grades in the mid-seventies with a lot of extra-curricular activities are better than grades in the eighties with no involvement.

## GMAT

The quantitative score is usually looked at closely, especially if an applicant does not have any university-level math courses and their work experience is not quantitative in nature.

Most schools put a significant amount of emphasis on the GMAT score. For schools who do not require a GMAT, see the chapter "Unique Characteristics."

## PERSONAL STATEMENTS

Some MBA schools require applicants to write an essay, or a detailed questionnaire, on why they want to do an MBA as part of their admission requirements. It is very important that applicants humbly sell themselves.

Point out what your strengths are and back them up with specific achievements. If you had an ordinary job, perhaps you had some innovative ideas and put them into practice.

Remember that in an MBA program part of the learning process comes from learning from your fellow students. Think of what unique characteristics or experiences you have had that might be an interesting addition to the mix.

When asked how the MBA could help you, or where you could improve, try to be believable. Picture someone reading hundreds and sometimes thousands of statements. After they have read comments like, "I work too hard," or "I set high standards so I get impatient with others," you can imagine how this type of comment can lose its credibility. Sometimes the best learning experiences are the result of failures. The following statement is more likely to be convincing: "I need to work on decision making and motivating people, and an MBA would help me to do this. I know if I could get a handle on that I would have more opportunities."

*Your statement should . . .*

- follow a logical argument and be well organized with no spelling or grammatical errors. The statement of purpose is not only used for content but as a check of writing skills.
- show that you have given it some serious thought even if you may not know exactly where you are heading.
- explain why you chose that particular MBA program.

*Avoid . . .*

- a generic letter.
- giving the impression that the MBA will be the solution of life's problems.
- showing a lack of direction, for example, having several degrees but never having put them to use.


## PRESENTATION OF RÉSUMÉ

Presentation is important. Avoid spelling mistakes and grammatical errors. Your résumé should be well organized and inviting to read.

The MBA program stresses group work. Evidence of interpersonal skills and people-oriented activities is important.

## LETTERS OF REFERENCE

This is the one requirement that can probably hurt you more than help you. The admissions committee is expecting to see glowing reports since this is something you have control over. Therefore, nice letters are deadly. Statements like, "I'm sure an MBA will give him/her every opportunity to improve him/herself," may be taken as a warning. A poor reference letter looks even worse because it shows poor judgement on the part of the applicant.

Do not assume everyone will give a good reference. Only choose people that you know will give you an *excellent* reference. Your references are supposed to be people who are on your side. Supply references with background information about you. Good letters are specific and measure results or achievements.

The best references are people who know you in a work or school environment. Work references can attest to your ability to get along with your colleagues, presentation skills, achievements, initiative, and problem-solving skills to name a few. School references can comment on leadership ability, working with others, logical thinking, and written and oral communication skills, as well as other abilities specific to your situation.

The most powerful effect occurs when all the references comment positively on the same characteristics, and there is a commonality of theme. Using people with powerful titles is less impressive than someone who has worked closely with you and can accurately evaluate you.

## INTERVIEWS

Most MBA schools use the interview to clarify information presented in the application package or to give marginal applicants another opportunity to present a stronger case. The interview could be used to ascertain interpersonal and communication skills or, in the case of foreign students, to evaluate their command of the school's working language.

Be careful. Interviews do not necessarily have to be conducted in person. A telephone call to ask a few questions is also an interview.

Be advised that there is no upper limit on what you can provide to build a better case.

# Consider This When Choosing an MBA School

## THE GEOGRAPHIC SETTING PLAYS A ROLE

If you want to work in an intense corporate setting in a large metropolitan area, consider the University of Toronto, McGill University, or the University of Calgary. Here, you can make contacts while working on projects involving the business community and get a feel for the lifestyle.

Universities that are far removed from major business centres will probably not get the variety or numbers of recruiters as will schools in larger cities. This will make your own job search even more critical.

## THE STUDENT PROFILE OF THE SCHOOL

A significant percentage of what you learn in an MBA program comes from your fellow students. Therefore, programs that require a number of years of work experience as part of their admission criteria will give you a richer experience. The average age of students can be a key indicator in this. If the school you choose admits a significant number of applicants straight out of undergraduate studies, you can make the most of this situation by taking night courses with the part-time students who will have more work experience.

## WHAT TEACHING STYLE HELPS
## YOU TO LEARN BEST

The teaching style can include lecture, case, projects, and simulations to name a few. The majority of schools strike a balance between lecture and case. On the continuum of lecture and case study, University of Western Ontario polarizes the case side, and the University of British Columbia leans largely toward the lecture side. Both schools use other teaching styles as well, but one dominates.

## DO YOU WANT AN AREA OF SPECIALTY
## OR GENERAL MANAGEMENT

Some school programs are highly structured, and others are not. For example, McMaster University has a number of concentration streams that are set out with required courses. Simon Fraser University fosters the development of specific expertise. Other schools such as Université de Sherbrooke, Memorial University of Newfoundland, and Université de Moncton do not offer concentrations. Perhaps you should consider a Master of Science in Management if you want an in-depth knowledge base (see Chart on Related Programs in the Appendix).

# University of Alberta

■ **INQUIRIES**

Associate Dean, MBA Program
Faculty of Business
University of Alberta
Edmonton, Alberta
T6G 2R6
(403) 492-3946

## FULL-TIME PROGRAM

■ **APPLICATION DEADLINE DATE FOR ADMISSIONS**

May 31

■ **REQUIRED TO SUBMIT**

- GMAT score
- Two official post-secondary transcripts
- TOEFL score is required from candidates whose first language is not English
- Three reference letters
- Statement of purpose one to two pages in length
- Detailed résumé is recommended

■ **AVERAGE GPA**

3.3/4.0 or B+ or 75%

■ **AVERAGE GMAT**

607
If the GMAT is written more than once, the best score is used

■ **PREFERENCE GIVEN TO A FOUR-YEAR DEGREE OVER A THREE-YEAR DEGREE?**

No

- **NUMBER OF APPLICANTS**
  284

- **SIZE OF INCOMING CLASS**
  31 (The 1990–91 class was small. Average enrolment is 55)

- **AVERAGE AGE OF STUDENTS**
  27

- **PERCENTAGE OF CLASS THAT ARE WOMEN**
  32%

- **PERCENTAGE OF CLASS WITH FULL-TIME WORK EXPERIENCE**
  78%

- **DISTRIBUTION OF UNDERGRADUATE DEGREES**

  | | |
  |---|---|
  | BSc 33% | BEd 3% |
  | BComm 25% | BMus 3% |
  | BA 24% | LLB 3% |
  | BSc Engineering 9% | |

- **OTHER RELATED PROGRAMS**
  BSc Engineering/MBA, MBA/LLB, MEng/MBA, Master of Health Services Administration, Master of Public Management, Master of Public Management/LLB, and a PhD in Business Management implemented in 1983

The MBA Program at the University of Alberta prides itself on being selective in its choice of students. The program targets individuals who can meet the rigorous demands of the program both intellectually and analytically. Maria David-Evans, MBA '92, states that "The quality of people who come out of the program are used to a high level of productivity." The program is tailored to mature individuals who possess good judgement, which usually comes from experience in the business world, and individuals who can lead and work with others effectively.

How does this translate into being admitted? Work experience is definitely an advantage. For students who are admitted directly from their undergraduate degree with no full-time work experience, the decision is based strictly on academic qualifications. Therefore more than the minimum requirements will be expected. Reference letters are looked at carefully to see if the individual has the ability to work with people since there is a significant amount of group work in the program. Extended periods of education with no work experience may be regarded as a lack of direction. Applicants do not have to know exactly what they want to do, but their statement of purpose should be well written and thought out.

Although it seems like a contradiction of terms, Terry Daniel, Associate Dean and Professor of the program, describes the MBA at the University of Alberta as based on a strong research program that is internationally recognized and pragmatic in nature with excellent teaching. Daniel comments that "The profs. are less geared to the here and now, and more able to adapt to the changing times." Three professors have won the 3M National Teaching Award Program for excellence. Maria David-Evans, MBA '92, comments on the high quality of teaching and describes it as having "three levels: theory, incorporating experiential learning process in application of theory, and an individual focus on improvement and evaluation of each student."

The structure of the program is unique in that nine of the ten courses in the first year of the MBA program are taught in common with the Master of Public Management Program. Daniel comments, "We see this as being a real strength to our program — to be sensitized to public management issues since the public sector is a big part of the Canadian business environment."

The MBA program at the University of Alberta definitely has a general management focus where breadth of course work is emphasized. No formal concentrations are either defined or encouraged. The majority of students opt for a non-thesis route. However, for students who want some focus, a thesis route is offered in their second year. The thesis has the weight of three courses and is researched and written under the supervision of an adviser and a thesis committee.

As to the focus of qualitative versus quantitative: Daniel states that University of Alberta's MBA falls "towards the quantitative end but not overly quantitative — to that side of centre." The University of Alberta calendar states, "Those who lack quantitative exposure are encouraged to undertake some preparatory work prior to entering the program." A university-level mathematics course with emphasis on introductory calculus and/or statistics is recommended.

The one area where Daniel would like to see the program improve is in its national and international representation of students. Currently the majority of students come from the province of Alberta. Don Cummings, MBA '91, mentions that "there are mostly local Albertans in the program with maybe six to eight foreign students." A few additional students are from other provinces in Canada.

## PART-TIME PROGRAM

■ **APPLICATION DEADLINE DATE FOR ADMISSIONS**
No formal deadline but applicants are encouraged to apply by
May 31 for September entry and November 1st for January
(only part-time students can enter the program in January)

■ **NUMBER OF APPLICANTS**
52

■ **SIZE OF INCOMING CLASS**
47

■ **AVERAGE AGE OF STUDENTS**
30

According to Daniel, "The requirements and rigour of the part-time program
are identical to the full-time. This is the wave of the future since students
are becoming more reluctant to take time out of their careers."

Part-time students in the MBA program at the University of Alberta have
five years to complete the program. All first-year courses are available at night
as well as in the day, and many second-year electives are also available at
night. There is flexibility in the program in that there is no minimum course
load. In 1990 the administration dropped their one semester (four month)
residency requirement for part-time students.

In September of 1991 delivery of the program will be made off-campus at
Ft. McMurray as well as in Edmonton. A contract has been made with
Syncrude for instructors to be on-site at Ft. McMurray one day a week for
successful Syncrude applicants. Employees from SUNCOR, hospitals, and other
firms will also have access to the program upon acceptance into the program.

## PLACEMENT

Career planning and recruitment are carried out by an in-house Office of
Placement Services. Seminars on résumé writing and interview techniques
are conducted; individual résumé and cover letter critiques are provided upon
request, mock interviews are available, and individual counselling is provided
as requested. A résumé book is published annually, and over seven hundred
copies are distributed to major corporations and government organizations.

To help students in their own job search, a salary and placement survey of the previous year's graduates is conducted. This information is provided to all graduate students in the Faculty in the fall of their graduating year.

The Placement Services were initiated five years ago, and some students feel that the placement function still has not reached its potential. Don Cummings, MBA '91, states, "The Placement service is one area of weakness — especially to students with no experience or only one or two years. There is more of a focus on undergraduate business students." He goes on to explain, "It is easy to place BComm students with Chartered Accountant firms or entry-level marketing positions, but you go back to do your MBA for different reasons." Despite these concerns, eighty per cent of graduates have jobs within two months of graduation.

The top-five companies in terms of numbers of offers last year were

- Bank of Nova Scotia
- Royal Bank
- Northern Telecom
- Government of Alberta
- Toronto-Dominion Bank

## ON EDMONTON

Linda Climenhaga, MBA '93, describes University of Alberta's campus as "a large campus with a real 'hodge podge' of architecture and buildings. We have everything from high-rises to turn-of-the-century original buildings to one in the shape of a turtle." Linda goes on to say that "This fits in with the personality of the city. There is a little bit of the old and a lot of the new. Edmonton's history only starts around 1890."

Sports facilities on-campus are excellent, and you can bike for miles through the river valley, which is quite beautiful. The campus is right on the river cliff.

The Faculty of Business is very proud of their new building opened in 1984. Full-time MBA students have designated individual study carrels, and all MBA students have access to their own lounge and excellent computing facilities. The business building is connected to the HUB mall, which is a combination shopping centre and apartment complex. The HUB, in turn, is connected to the main Rutherford Library. The business reference division, however, is conveniently housed in the Winspear Reading Room, located in the Faculty of Business Building. In other words, going outside in the winter is not all that necessary.

Accommodation averages around $450 for a two-bedroom apartment or $650 for a two-bedroom apartment in a high-rise. Residence accommodation on-campus is also available.

The North Saskatchewan river divides the city of Edmonton into north and south. The campus is across the bridge and about a fifteen-minute walk from downtown. The Light Rail Transit is expanding to the south side of the city and will link the campus much more directly and quickly to downtown. Hopefully it will relieve the parking problem on-campus, which is very frustrating at present.

## STUDENT PROFILES

*SUSAN DELANEY*
MBA '91

* Full-time student in the MBA program
* Four-year BA in Psychology from the University of Alberta in 1989
* Looking for a marketing position in the manufactured goods or services area in Alberta
* Home town Stony Plain, Alberta
* Single

"I looked at a lot of schools, but I was very impressed with the quality of teachers at U. of A.," comments Susan. In addition, Susan received a $4,000 graduate assistanceship for working six hours per week for two terms. These factors made Susan decide in favour of doing her MBA at the University of Alberta.

Susan was one of the few students who was admitted to the MBA program without full-time work experience.

"It was hard to get used to being one of the youngest in the class," says Susan. At social events fellow students would "introduce me to their wives and little kids or kids that were older than you are." Susan also mentions that she was one of only twelve women in her full-time class.

"It is an entirely different way of learning," comments Susan when she compares the MBA to her undergraduate Psychology degree. "In Psychology there were thirteen in my graduating class, and it was all seminars, whereas the MBA is mostly lecture and quantitative."

How did she get through it? "We have a very tight class, and we banded together and got through it as a group."

In Susan's opinion, "First year is very quantitative; more than it has to be." She describes first year as "very stressful. They don't let you know that you'll be all right unless you really screw up. In second year the work is the same difficulty, but you have more papers and assignments rather than exams, and you know you will be okay."

"I think the MBA has helped me. Maybe not right now in terms of getting a job immediately, but I have gained a lot. People in the city respect the degree."


*BRAD SONNENBERG*
MBA '91

- Part-time then full-time student in the MBA program
- Four-year BSc in Electrical Engineering from the University of Alberta in 1981
- Worked for Ed TEL, most recently as Project Engineer
- Currently on leave to finish his MBA (Ed TEL is not paying tuition or books)
- Starts a new job with Ed TEL as a Senior Business Analyst after graduating with his MBA
- Home town Pibroch, Alberta, 100 km north of Edmonton
- Married, with no children

"When I started the program part-time, there was a residency requirement, so I planned to do my last term full-time. When they changed the rule last year, I didn't feel like changing my plans," comments Brad.

Brad was in a unique position of being able to compare full-time and part-time since he attended the MBA program at University of Alberta in both capacities.

"Going part-time you get a more mature class with work experience, but you don't develop a close relationship with them, whereas full-time students almost live and breathe together and build stronger relationships with classmates and professors."

In Brad's opinion the biggest strength of the MBA comes from the interaction with the other students who have work experience because you learn from their applications. Brad went so far as to say that "This was even more important than the professors or academic content."

Although Brad was generally pleased with the program he has one major complaint. "I'm constantly amazed that they [the faculty and administration] don't have the slightest idea of who their customers are. I'm talking to bureaucrats. No business would survive this way. For example, administrative offices are not open at noon, profs. only want to teach between 8:30 and 4 p.m."

Brad says, "There are some professors who are very good, but there are too many whose priorities are totally on research." Is he glad he did his MBA? "Yes. I came from a very technical background in the labs in engineering software and hardware, and I tended not to interact with people but was isolated." Brad continues, "The program has had a tremendous effect on me. I tend to look at situations with the whole picture now. It's not a gold card to the world of business, but it has changed my thinking."

# University of British Columbia

---

■ **INQUIRIES**

MBA Program
Faculty of Commerce and Business Administration
University of British Columbia
2053 Main Mall
Vancouver, British Columbia
V6T 1Y8
(604) 822-8422

## FULL-TIME PROGRAM

■ **APPLICATION DEADLINE DATE FOR ADMISSIONS**

15 May

■ **REQUIRED TO SUBMIT**

- GMAT score
- Official post-secondary transcripts
- TOEFL score of 600 is required from candidates whose first language is not English
- Three reference letters, at least two of which should be academic
- Personal statement
- Résumé is optional

■ **AVERAGE GPA**

Minimum GPA is 3.0 or B or 72% at the University of British Columbia or whatever per cent a B is at the applicant's undergraduate university. The average is based on the final two years of senior level coursework and must include a minimum of four A's.

■ **AVERAGE GMAT**

610 (Minimum GMAT accepted is 550)
If the GMAT is written more than once, the best score is used.

Applicants are expected to write the GMAT no later than the March sitting.

■ **PREFERENCE GIVEN TO A FOUR-YEAR DEGREE OVER A THREE-YEAR DEGREE?**

Three-year degrees are not considered unless the student has first-class standing and work experience.

■ **NUMBER OF APPLICANTS**

780 (after pre-screening)

■ **SIZE OF INCOMING CLASS**

144

■ **AVERAGE AGE OF STUDENTS**

26

■ **PERCENTAGE OF CLASS THAT ARE WOMEN**

29%

■ **PERCENTAGE OF CLASS WITH FULL-TIME WORK EXPERIENCE**

Work experience is preferred but not required. Specific data was not available. However, rarely are students straight out of undergraduate programs admitted if only minimum requirements are met.

■ **DISTRIBUTION OF UNDERGRADUATE DEGREES**

BBA/BComm 32%          BA 10%
BSc Engineering 21%     Other Undergraduate 10%
BSc 18%                 BA Economics 9%

■ **OTHER RELATED PROGRAMS**

MBA/LLB, a Master of Science in Business Administration, and the largest PhD program in Business Administration in Canada. In September 1991 the first class will be admitted in a Master in Advanced Technology Management offered jointly with the School of Engineering.

After fourteen years, Peter Lusztig has stepped down from the position of Dean of the Faculty of Commerce and Business Administration. Lusztig was the longest-serving dean in the faculty's history.

Michael Goldberg, Professor of Urban Land Policy in the Faculty of

Commerce and Business Administration, began his six-year term on 1 July 1991. In the University of British Columbia's press release on 7 December 1990, President David Strangway describes Goldberg as a "distinguished scholar with an international reputation in the field of housing and urban land economics. He has made the University of British Columbia urban land economics group one of the pre-eminent groups in the world and has served the community very well." Goldberg's areas of research include the development of international financial centres, globalization of real property markets, housing economics, and urban land markets. Goldberg is currently Chair of the British Columbia Real Estate Foundation and a Commissioner of the British Columbia Housing Management Commission.

Under Lusztig's deanship, the direction of the Faculty of Commerce and Business Administration had been "to follow the Massachusetts Institute of Technology and the University of Chicago's examples and concentrate more on the theoretical approach and try to make our mark there," explains Lusztig in Peter Newman's article in the 15 September 1986 issue of *Maclean's*. In the 28 May 1990 issue of the *Financial Post* Greg Kinch states, "Business education in Canada is often described as a continuum, with Western and its practical MBA teaching orientation on one end; and UBC with its reputation for academic research on the other. All other schools are judged according to these models." The new direction under the leadership of Goldberg will be followed with interest but it is not expected to change.

The University of British Columbia is Canada's second largest university. The average class size in the first year of the MBA program is held to thirty-five, decreasing to between fifteen and twenty in second year. Over ninety electives are available for students to choose from.

The MBA Program is a general management degree as opposed to the more specialized Master of Science in Business Administration. However, students enrolled in the MBA can concentrate their areas of study in Accounting, Arts Administration, Business Statistics, Finance, Industrial Relations, International Business, Management Information Systems, Management Science, Marketing, Organizational Behaviour, Policy Analysis, Small Enterprise Development, Transportation and Logistics, and Urban Land Economics.

Arts Administration is the newest option offered in the MBA Program. The University of British Columbia calendar describes it as a program "for those seeking a high level of administrative skill specifically suited to museums, galleries, performing arts and similar organizations." Unique administrative problems faced by arts organizations, business functional areas as applied to arts organizations, and cultural policy issues are addressed by specialized seminars. In addition, a three-month internship in an arts organization is required.

An international focus of the MBA program at the University of British Columbia can be attributed to its location, the establishment of one of the Centres for International Business, and student exchange programs. The school's geographic location attracts a significant number of students from abroad. Approximately one-fifth of the students enrolled in the MBA class are from other countries, especially from the Pacific Rim countries. Over half of the students are from locations other than British Columbia. Also, Vancouver is in a key location in relation to the Pacific Rim's economic and commercial development. The Centre for International Business Studies (CIBS) is funded by the Department of External Affairs and contributions obtained from private sector organizations. The mandate of the CIBS is to promote research in the field of international business and trade, award scholarships, and give the opportunity for hands-on research experience. Support for International Business also comes from the Provincial Government and the private sector.

Since 1984 the University of British Columbia has participated in exchange programs abroad. Currently exchange programs are established with leading universities in Australia, Austria, Belgium, Denmark, France, Hong Kong, Hungary, Italy, Korea, The Netherlands, Singapore, and The United Kingdom. Second-year students can apply to spend one term studying in another country. "While University of British Columbia students are away on exchange, the exchange universities send their MBA's to replace the UBC students on exchange. This provides an expanded international flavour to UBC's program," describes the University of British Columbia's calendar.

On the continuum of quantitative versus qualitative, Lusztig describes the University of British Columbia's MBA program as being closer to the quantitative end. Only quite basic Math is required. The calendar states that "The program emphasizes analytical skills and the ability to apply the appropriate techniques to the evaluation of alternatives, economic analysis, and strategy formulation." A remedial quantitative methods course is offered in the summer term prior to the beginning of the program in September.

Shannon Taylor, MBA '89, came into the program with an arts background in psychology. "I would warn any students with an arts background that the MBA program at UBC is very analytical and quantitative. I found the courses very challenging, especially in first year when I was taking accounting, decision analysis, and micro economics," comments Shannon.

Students with previous academic backgrounds in any of the core-course areas can be granted exemptions by writing the exemption exams prior to the beginning of the MBA program. Exemptions are granted on a course-by-course basis. Quantitative methods and Economics can be granted exemptions on the basis of transcripts. Exemptions for all other courses are determined by exemption examinations. For recent Bachelor of Commerce graduates with a first-class average in their final two years and a GMAT score above 620, there is a good possibility that all first-year courses may be waived, allowing the applicant to directly enter second year.

## PART-TIME PROGRAM

■ **NUMBER OF APPLICANTS**
   94 (after pre-screening)

■ **SIZE OF INCOMING CLASS**
   45

■ **AVERAGE AGE OF STUDENTS**
   29

■ **PERCENTAGE OF CLASS THAT ARE WOMEN**
   33%

The MBA program at the University of British Columbia is also offered on a part-time basis. Courses are offered in the evening during three terms each year: September to December, January to April, and May to July. Students are required to complete a minimum of four courses during these three terms. Students should complete the degree within two to five years, depending on their background. First-year classes are held in the evening only. Second-year classes are offered in both day or night classes.

## PLACEMENT

The Faculty's placement service works in conjunction with the Canada Employment Centre (CEC) on campus to provide placement and counselling services to business students. Seminars are presented each year on résumé preparation and interview techniques. The business community is often called upon to participate in mock interviews or to act as speakers.

The placement service and the CEC facilitate on-campus recruiting. Last year over three hundred firms recruited business graduates and students for permanent career opportunities as well as summer positions. In addition, the Commerce Graduate Society produces a résumé brochure of MBA/MSc graduates that is sent to over four hundred companies for their recruitment use.

## ON VANCOUVER

The University of British Columbia is built on the westernmost point of the city of Vancouver. From the university's campus the view is breathtaking. The campus spreads over a promontory surrounded by the Pacific Ocean and is overlooked by towering mountains. The parkland forest acts as a buffer between the campus and the residential area. The campus is approximately a half-hour bus ride from downtown.

Housing is expensive and can be difficult to find so you may be advised to start your hunt for accommodations in July for September. Graduate residences and a condominium complex are available on-campus but they often have a waiting list. If you are interested, you might consider applying for on-campus accommodation when you apply for admission.

Debbie Intas, MBA '90, describes Vancouver as "the most beautiful city in the world. There are parks everywhere, and it is an outdoor person's dream." Not only does a year-round temperate climate permit full enjoyment of outdoor living, but it is indeed possible to ski in the morning, sail in the afternoon, and enjoy a concert in the evening of the same day. The pace of life is described as "laid back."

## STUDENT PROFILES*

*STEVE BAILLIE*
MBA '89

- Completed the MBA program on a full-time basis
- Five-year Honours BSc degree in Physics (co-op program) from the University of Victoria in 1986
- Worked in research with the Atomic Energy of Canada Limited in Pinawa, Manitoba, before entering his MBA
- Presently employed with Citibank of Canada as a Senior Associate, financial analyst in the corporate finance group
- Home town Victoria
- Single

After researching MBA programs, Steve decided on the University of British

---

* Note: Only alumni were interviewed in compliance with the University of British Columbia's position that students not be contacted.

Columbia. "UBC was ranked in the top three for what I wanted to do — specialize in finance."

One of the strengths of the program, in Steve's opinion, was the finance courses and the fact that there was more lecture-style teaching than case. "I would rather learn by the classroom method, especially for corporate finance courses," comments Steve.

During the first term of his second year, Steve attended the London School of Business. It cost him less to go to England than if he had attended the University of British Columbia that term because of a scholarship that the University of British Columbia brought to his attention.

Steve gained a more international perspective. "I learned more specifics about European business — for example, the English tax system — and I got a different viewpoint on the 1992 integration of the Common Market than if I had stayed in Canada."

In Steve's opinion, being away for the first term of his final year put him at a disadvantage in terms of the job search. He found that recruitment is heaviest in the first term, but the placement people were very supportive.

Regarding the recruitment process in general, Steve comments, "Being so far away from Toronto and considering the size of UBC, we don't get a lot of the big corporations recruiting on-campus." He went on to describe the outlook at the University of British Columbia's finance department. "The lifestyle tends to be non-corporate. I was one of the minority that decided to go the high finance corporate route."

"I am very happy with where I am due to a little bit of luck, good recruitment with Citibank of Canada, and a good grounding in finance from UBC. There is no way I would be here if I didn't have my MBA," states Steve.


*DEBBIE INTAS*
MBA '90

- Completed the MBA program on a full-time basis
- Three-year BComm from McGill University in 1985
- Worked for Monark Sports Ltd. in the marketing of Elan skies
- Currently employed by the Royal Bank of Canada as an Introductory Accounts Management Trainee/Corporate Banking
- Home town Montreal
- Single

Before deciding on the University of British Columbia's MBA program, Debbie reviewed several Canadian, American, and European programs. She finally narrowed it down between the London School of Business and the University of British Columbia.

Debbie chose UBC because she felt it was strong in finance, International Business, and Organizational Behaviour, and finance was Debbie's area of interest. Also, "I was advised that if I wanted to work in Canada, I should do my degree in Canada."

Debbie felt strongly that a strength of the program was that "There was no one type of student in the program." The student population was diverse in terms of nationality, age, and undergraduate backgrounds.

Debbie was also very pleased with the quality of teaching. "Some professors I'll probably remember for the rest of my life. I use some of the material I learned every day. I had professors from Singapore, Japan, and the United States, and they instilled in me a desire to learn, to stay up until four in the morning working."

When asked where the program could improve, Debbie comments that the University of British Columbia had weak ties with the business community. "You go to university for the academics but you also want the network and to be able to work with more businesses on projects."

The MBA has definitely helped Debbie. Through group work, "You learn to work with people, and you are forced to deal with them like you are in the work place."

# University of Calgary

■ **INQUIRIES**

The Admissions Committee
MBA Program
Faculty of Management
University of Calgary
2500 University Drive North West
Calgary, Alberta
T2N 1N4
(403) 220-3808

## FULL-TIME PROGRAM

■ **APPLICATION DEADLINE DATE FOR ADMISSIONS**

15 January if you wish to be considered for scholarships
31 May

■ **REQUIRED TO SUBMIT**

- GMAT score
- Official post-secondary transcripts
- TOEFL score is required from candidates whose first language is not English
- Three reference letters
- Personal statement
- Résumé

■ **AVERAGE GPA**

3.3/4.0 (Minimum GPA is 3.0/4.0) or B+ or 75%

■ **AVERAGE GMAT**

604 (Minimum is 500)
If the GMAT is written more than once, the scores are not averaged

- **PREFERENCE GIVEN TO A FOUR-YEAR DEGREE OVER A THREE-YEAR DEGREE?**
  No

- **NUMBER OF APPLICANTS**
  420 including both full-time and part-time

- **SIZE OF INCOMING CLASS**
  60

- **AVERAGE AGE OF STUDENTS**
  31 average including both full-time and part-time

- **PERCENTAGE OF CLASS THAT ARE WOMEN**
  33%

- **PERCENTAGE OF CLASS WITH FULL-TIME WORK EXPERIENCE**
  100% (Average length of work experience is eight years; minimum required is three years)

- **DISTRIBUTION OF UNDERGRADUATE DEGREES**
  BSc 34%                    BSc Engineering 18%
  BBA/BComm 21%              Other Undergraduate 7%
  BA Social Science 20%

- **OTHER RELATED PROGRAMS**
  PhD

While some MBA programs are perpetuating the myth that management is all analysis, the University of Calgary is working very hard to put a stop to the myth. "U. of C.'s MBA program is making a push towards trying to emphasize the implementation side of management," states Jess Chua, Associate Dean.

"Live projects" are used as the major vehicle for the shift of focus to implementation. "Live projects" are actual problems that businesses in the local community are experiencing and have approached University of Calgary's faculty in the MBA program for assistance.

Why not use cases? Cases and lectures are used, primarily in first year to teach concepts. In second year "live projects" are emphasized more because, in Chua's opinion, cases tend to be unrealistic. "Cases give students all the data in one place, and identifies the problems for them. In real life people only tell you the symptoms."

Chua credits the success of the implementation approach to the maturity and experience of the students in the program. "Companies are getting value out of it," states Chua. Calgary, Western Canada's leading head-office centre, also provides a tremendous opportunity for interaction.

One of the benefits of emphasizing implementation is that it causes a change of attitude in the students, comments Chua. "After you decide what has to be done, what do you do? Suddenly they realize that they don't know — but the CEO does. It makes the MBA student more humble and willing to learn."

Students can choose a general management focus at the University of Calgary or they can choose to concentrate in an area of specialization. Concentrations consisting of a maximum of three half courses in an area of study are available in Accounting and Information Systems, Entrepreneurship and Venture Development, Management of Financial Resources, Management of Human Resources, Management of Public Institutions, Marketing and Distribution Systems, Operations Management, Project Management, and Tourism and Hospitality Management. A thesis option is also possible.

During the admission process a "people orientation" is stressed. If a candidate has an absence of people-oriented activities this may be a cause for concern. Another red flag may be a very high GMAT score but no people skills outlined in the résumé.

On the positive side, the GMAT score is not broken into quantitative and qualitative categories. "We have admitted people who have just barely met the minimum requirements but have great people skills," comments Chua. A holistic evaluation of a person's potential to be a manager is checked by the reference letters, statement of purpose, the résumé, and occasionally an interview.

Although the part-time program at the University of Calgary is sixteen years old, the full-time program is only five years old. The youth of the program supports the school's innovation.


## PART-TIME PROGRAM


### ■ SIZE OF INCOMING CLASS
60

Students enrolled in the part-time program at the University of Calgary have a maximum time limit of six years to complete their degree. There is flexibility in the program in that there is no minimum course load required and students can pay per course. There is not much integration of part-time and full-time students since part-time courses are held mostly in the evening. Part-time students can request day-time classes if space permits.


## PLACEMENT

The Faculty of Management maintains its own Career Development Office (CDO) separate from the university-wide Canada Employment Centre. Its mandate is to facilitate the job search for both undergraduate and graduate business students. The CDO is housed in Scurfield Hall, the new multi-million-dollar business building, which opened in January 1986.

The CDO is equipped with interview rooms, resource material on job-search techniques and company files. Seminars on résumé writing and interviewing skills are offered as well as a mock interview program conducted by recruitment officers from the business community.

Job opportunities are maintained on a computer database, which can be accessed through the mainframe. Also a network of alumni is maintained to be used as a resource of possible mentors.


## ON CALGARY

The atmosphere of Calgary and its business community is one of a keen entrepreneurial spirit resulting from the dramatic change in its economic base from ranching to petroleum exploration and development.

The University of Calgary's campus is located on the outskirts of the downtown core. The new Light Rail Transit can get you downtown in fifteen minutes or you can take the bus and be there in a half an hour. Transportation in general is excellent in Calgary. The streets are laid out in a grid pattern so you can find your way around easily and quickly. Greg Molaro, MBA '91, comments that "I live ten to fifteen miles on the other side of town but it only takes me twenty-two minutes to get to campus. There is no deterrent for living farther away from campus."

Calgary is famous for its Chinooks. Shirley van de Wetering jokingly comments, "If you don't like the weather just wait ten minutes. You have to have your boots, umbrella, and sweater because you never know what it's going to be like." About an hour's drive to the west there is terrific skiing in the Rocky Mountains.

The University of Calgary's new business building — Scurfield Hall — is the envy of most business schools in Canada. The aura of big business is everywhere as you walk into the "Shell Room" and the "Dome Room," etc. Most of the funding for the building was provided by donations from individuals and corporations who sometimes sponsored classrooms. A management skill development laboratory with break-out rooms for group discussions, discussion syndicate rooms, formal and informal conference rooms, and computer laboratories are a few of the specialized facilities of Scurfield Hall. It also has its own cafeteria, dining room, copy centre, and audio-visual centre.

MBA students have their own study room nicknamed the "Bubble," which has individual carrels. Only MBA students have the keys to it.


## STUDENT PROFILES

*BOB BREWS*
MBA '92

- Part-time student in the MBA program
- Four-year Honours BA in Philosophy from Queen's University in 1974; one-year Bachelor of Journalism from Carleton in 1975
- Worked for the CBC in Ottawa and Calgary
- Presently working for the family business in electrical wholesaling as Vice-President and General Manager
- Intends to carry on with the family business
- Home town Calgary
- Married, with one child

Bob wanted to continue working while he did his MBA part-time. "Even though I didn't have a lot of choice, the program at the University of Calgary was what I wanted. It's practical and has a general-management orientation. I was looking for a broad management point of view so I could supervise the specialist more effectively."

Bob describes the faculty at the University of Calgary as having "useful insights," being "very knowledgeable," and they "listened to students." One professor that Bob, and other students who were interviewed, felt was an exceptional professor was Jim Graham who teaches New Ventures. Bob explains that "He helps a lot of people long after they graduate."

In Bob's opinion most of the courses are project oriented with the exception of the Management Information Systems Department. Bob states that "They are the weakest department in the school both in the way they structure their courses and the way they approach the students."

Overall, Bob has found that "Every course I've taken has had an immediate practical application to my business, some of which I could even attach dollar values to."


## SHIRLEY VAN DE WETERING
MBA '91

- Part-time then full-time student in the MBA program
- Four-year BSc in Physical Geography and Resource Management from the University of Victoria in 1983
- Worked in Calgary for five years with a law firm in a research capacity
- Areas of interest are marketing and new ventures, but she is uncertain as to what her next step will be
- Home town Kamloops
- Married, no children

"I don't feel cut off from the business community. It doesn't feel like I'm at school, and the real world is out there," explained Shirley. In Shirley's opinion the Dean of the MBA program and the faculty are well connected to the business community.

Some of the examples she gave of this close relationship were the management advisory committee and the Venture Forum series, where they invite small business owners and corporations to address a theme such as growth strategy.

However, she felt that the school could improve in one area. "Between the foundation and core courses there is some repetition in the areas of Human Resources, Operations Management, and Information Systems. I would like to see some combination of these at the core level and more electives."

Having been enrolled in the program since 1988, Shirley has seen evidence of the administration listening to the concerns of part-time students. Accessibility to the administrative office, in the Faculty of Management, has been extended on Monday to 6:30 p.m. This is helpful since night classes start at 6:30 p.m. Also they are offering a few more courses in the spring term.

Doing the MBA program has helped Shirley because in her opinion, "As a female I needed an MBA since the Calgary community is highly technical and male dominated with oil and gas organizations."

# Concordia University

- **INQUIRIES**

  The Director
  MBA Program
  Concordia University
  1455 boulevard de Maisonneuve Ouest
  Suite GM 201-09
  Montréal, Québec
  H3G 1M8
  (514) 848-2717

## FULL-TIME PROGRAM

- **APPLICATION DEADLINE DATE FOR ADMISSIONS**

  28 February for Summer entry
  30 March for September entry
  30 October for January entry

- **REQUIRED TO SUBMIT**
  - GMAT score
  - Official post-secondary transcripts
  - TOEFL score is required from candidates whose first language is not English
  - Three reference letters (one academic)
  - Statement of purpose
  - Résumé and proof of Canadian citizenship

- **AVERAGE GPA**

  3.0 or B or 70%

- **AVERAGE GMAT**

  560–580
  If the GMAT is written more than once, the best score is used

Culture and language factors are taken into consideration for francophones

■ **PREFERENCE GIVEN TO A FOUR-YEAR DEGREE OVER A THREE-YEAR DEGREE?**
No

■ **NUMBER OF APPLICANTS**
531 in total  [ Summer 37 – Fall 402 – Winter 92 ]

■ **SIZE OF INCOMING CLASS**
87 in total  [ Summer 9 – Fall 59 – Winter 19 ]

■ **AVERAGE AGE OF STUDENTS**
26–28

■ **PERCENTAGE OF CLASS THAT ARE WOMEN**
Approximately 35–40%

■ **PERCENTAGE OF CLASS WITH FULL-TIME WORK EXPERIENCE**
90% (Average length of work experience is four years)

■ **DISTRIBUTION OF UNDERGRADUATE DEGREES**

| | |
|---|---|
| BSc 27% | BSc Engineering 19% |
| BA 24% | Other Undergraduate 12% |
| BComm 18% | |

■ **OTHER RELATED PROGRAMS**
Executive MBA Program, MSc in Administration, and PhD in Management

Concordia University's MBA program is of a generalist nature where inter-disciplinary and practical applications are stressed. In the words of Cleveland Patterson, Academic Director, MBA, "The program is very conceptual and rigorous but it has to be applied. The admission requirements stress work experience and maturity since the pedagogy of the program puts students in a position where they learn from one another."

Concordia does stress work experience. Four to five years is the average. Eighty per cent of the class of ninety had more than two years work experience. Applicants with a Bachelor of Commerce undergraduate degree must have a minimum of two-years work experience to be considered.

Applicants from other disciplines could be granted admission with less. Major changes affecting admissions requirements and the overall program have been decided on and will be implemented September 1991. Most affected by the new admission requirements will be the advanced standing. Prior to the review, applicants with a BBA/BCom or other undergraduate degree could apply for advance standing for parts or all of first year, depending on their academic background.

However, now there will be no advanced standing offered to applicants even if they have a Bachelor of Commerce undergraduate degree. If the applicant's grades are good enough, they may get an exemption, but they will have to substitute other courses. Substitute courses may be selected from the courses within the program although, Patterson notes, students will be "strongly urged to take courses outside the school of business."

The rational behind this change in policy, Patterson comments, is that "The MBA is not simply an accelerated Commerce degree." This policy puts Concordia in alignment with other top schools that tend not to give advance standing. In addition, it is a recognition that successful executives require a breadth of education that extends beyond traditional management courses.

In an attempt to create a homogeneous background for students coming from a variety of different undergraduate degrees, three qualifying modules will be held three to four weeks prior to the beginning of classes. There will be one in computing and two in mathematics. Exemptions from the math module will be made if it can be shown that a comparable math course has already been taken. The computer module will be mandatory for everyone to ensure familiarity with Concordia's computing facilities.

A further emphasis of the practical aspects of the MBA will be made. There will be more emphasis on managerial skills and human skills without jeopardizing the theory or the rigorous nature of the program. Three new modules will be introduced, covering topics such as working effectively in groups, conflict management, communication skills, and negotiating skills. Each module will be worth one credit. The modular nature will allow more flexibility in timing "so you can put it in the right place at the right time," Patterson states. These modules will be eleven hours each in length and may be held on a Saturday.

New and mandatory courses will be offered in the second year of the program in International Business (an interdisciplinary course) and Strategy and the External Environment. A mandatory research paper worth six credits and a research methodology course have always been compulsory. Now students will be given the option in 1992 to have a practicum: a group of students will be assigned to a firm for an in-depth consulting job (e.g., a business plan for a new product).

Concordia's MBA remains a rigorous graduate-level program but with more implementation built into it. The tuition freeze of twenty years has been lifted in the Province of Quebec, but tuition is still very reasonable when compared to the rest of Canada.

## PART-TIME PROGRAM

■ **NUMBER OF APPLICANTS**
    336 in total  [ Summer 49 – Fall 198 – Winter 89 ]

■ **SIZE OF INCOMING CLASS**
    89 in total  [ Summer 11 – Fall 49 – Winter 29 ]

Part-time students in Concordia's MBA program have a maximum time limit of seven years to complete the program. The majority of part-time students take classes in the evening, although it is possible to take courses during the day. Evening classes are scheduled from 5:30–8:30 p.m. or 8:30–11:30 p.m. The tri-semester format adds to the flexibility of the program.

The part-time students who were interviewed appreciated the fact that most of the people in the evening classes were older and had work experience. Peter Gandell, MBA '96, mentions, "I feel out of place with twenty-year-old full-time students." And Antony Gentilcore, MBA '91, comments, "I like part-time better than full-time because of the quality of students in terms of their experience. You learn much more."

## PLACEMENT

The School of Business has an in-house placement co-ordinator who facilitates on-campus recruiting. Also, each year an *MBA Profile Book* is published and distributed to several hundred companies across Canada. Concordia's Guidance Services complements the in-house placement function by offering individual and group counselling and Job Hunting Workshops specifically designed for MBA students.

The top-five companies in terms of numbers of offers last year were

- Canadian Pacific
- Glaxo Pharmaceutical
- Hewlett-Packard
- Laurentian Bank
- Royal Bank of Canada

## ON MONTREAL

The city of Montreal has a European flavour. People converse in French and other languages as well as English. Both Concordia University and McGill University are in the heart of the city. Concordia's school of business is split between three buildings, all within about three blocks of each other along de Maisonneuve, one of the main downtown streets. McGill University is a fifteen-minute walk away.

There is no shortage of affordable housing or reasonable little cafés and European restaurants. When asked about the winters in Montreal, the students always answered a resounding "very cold."

## STUDENT PROFILES

*SAMANTHA CRAMER*
MBA '91

* Full-time student in the MBA program
* Four-year BA in English Literature from Skidmore College, Saratoga Springs, NY, in 1986
* Worked for Harry Rosen as a visual sales associate for a year and then with a small computer resource company for six months
* Wants to work with an environmental consulting firm on the communication or marketing aspect
* Home town Montreal
* Single

Even after she graduated from her undergraduate degree, Samantha continued to take courses. She worked on her business certificate at Concordia and her management certificate at McGill.

After comparing her experiences at both universities, she chose Concordia for her MBA. Samantha enjoyed the friendly atmosphere at Concordia. "Work experience is very heavily weighted [at Concordia] whereas McGill has much more standardized boundaries. At Concordia my quantitative and qualitative were taken into account."

When asked what she liked most about the program at Concordia, Samantha mentions that "The group work here is very good. You have to work with other people to get your work done. It is similar to the high stress work environment on the job." Communication skills are also stressed.

Samantha says, "We are starting to do a lot of presentations. In every class, no matter what it is in, you have to do one."

In Samantha's opinion, the one area where Concordia's MBA program could improve would be in the marketing of its program to employers. When Samantha mentioned to people that she was working on her MBA she said she often got the response of "Oh, you're doing your MBA at McGill." She felt that there was more recruitment at McGill and that the general public was not very aware of Concordia's MBA program.


## ANTHONY GENTILCORE
### MBA '91

- Part-time student in the MBA program
- Three-year BSc in Computer Science from Concordia University in 1986
- While going to school part-time, he works as a manager of an information centre
- Company sponsors him and pays eighty per cent of his tuition
- French is mother tongue
- Home town Repentigny, Quebec, an eastern suburb of Montreal
- Married, with an infant

Anthony had the choice of either going to Concordia or McGill to do his MBA since he was admitted at both with entrance scholarships. He chose Concordia because, "By asking around, I heard it was less theoretical and more applied, more case work and more team work. I also knew the place because I did my undergraduate there."

Although Anthony started full-time he transferred to part-time after only six weeks. "I liked part-time better than full-time because the quality of student was higher in terms of their experience, and I learned much more." One disadvantage to part-time however is that some of the classes are scheduled from 8:30–11:30 p.m., which makes for a very long day.

In Anthony's opinion, Concordia has a very qualified finance department.

On the lighter side, the part-time and full-time student life is active, with lots of events including sports and a yearly barbecue to name a few.

Anthony does complain about the facilities. There is no centralized building. Classes are spread out between three buildings all within a couple of blocks of each other in the downtown core of Montreal. The library is poor, but soon it will be replaced by the one that is currently being built.

# Dalhousie University

■ **INQUIRIES**
School of Business Administration
Dalhousie University
6152 Coburg Road
Halifax, Nova Scotia
B3H 1Z5
(902) 494-7080

## *FULL-TIME PROGRAM*

■ **APPLICATION DEADLINE DATE FOR ADMISSIONS**
31 May strongly recommended
31 March for foreign students
Applications will not be processed after 15 July

■ **REQUIRED TO SUBMIT**
- GMAT score
- Two official post-secondary transcripts from each post-secondary institution attended
- TOEFL score is required from candidates whose first language is not English
- Two reference letters
- Two copies of personal statement
- Two copies of your résumé

■ **AVERAGE GPA**
3.3 or B+ or 75%

■ **AVERAGE GMAT**
580
If the GMAT is written more than once, all scores are considered; however, it is not policy to average the scores

- **PREFERENCE GIVEN TO A FOUR-YEAR DEGREE OVER A THREE-YEAR DEGREE?**

  Not compulsory, although seventy-five per cent of students have more than three years of post-secondary education.

- **NUMBER OF APPLICANTS**

  600

- **SIZE OF INCOMING CLASS**

  100

- **AVERAGE AGE OF STUDENTS**

  26

- **PERCENTAGE OF CLASS THAT ARE WOMEN**

  40%

- **PERCENTAGE OF CLASS WITH FULL-TIME WORK EXPERIENCE**

  50%

- **DISTRIBUTION OF UNDERGRADUATE DEGREES**

  BSc and BSc Engineering 46%   Other Undergraduate 3%
  BA 27%                        BEd 1%
  BBA/BComm 27%

- **GRADUATE DEGREES**

  4%

- **OTHER RELATED PROGRAMS**

  MBA/LLB, Master of Library Science and Information Studies (MLIS), Master of Public Administration, Master of Public Administration/LLB

The biggest myth surrounding Dalhousie University is that Dalhousie is a regional school oriented towards the Maritimes. In fact twenty to twenty-five per cent of the student body are from Ontario, and there are Dalhousie graduates in Toronto and all over Canada.

Dalhousie's incoming class is approximately one hundred in number, which puts it in the mid-size category of Canadian business schools. However, Dalhousie is the largest and perhaps the best-known MBA school of the east. Class size remains relatively small with numbers of around forty.

The professors, deans, and administration were described as very approachable, and students were known on a first-name basis. Almost all the students interviewed commented on how involved the faculty were with the business sector. Professors were actively consulting on a part-time basis, had considerable work experience before joining the faculty, or both.

A computing background is not a requirement of Dalhousie's Business School but the use of computers is integrated into all aspects of the curriculum. According to Eileen MacDougall, Co-ordinator, Student and Public Relations, "The MBA program will teach students how to use computers as a tool, not to become programmers. Therefore students will be taught word processing, dBASE, Lotus, etc." Computers are integrated into every course. Students either use them to analyze data, or as word processors, or to run simulation packages. According to Karen Radford, MBA '91, "My fellow students said that maybe we should buy a computer, and I didn't even know how to turn one on, but they have a two-day workshop and private tutorials. Now I feel quite comfortable." There is no formal math requirement, but some evidence of proficiency will be looked for.

Why would you choose to go to Dalhousie? Joseph Macdonald, MBA '91, describes the program as having "a strong generalist base with the opportunity to develop a specialization." It is possible to concentrate your studies by choosing your electives in areas such as finance, accounting, marketing, management information systems, and international business.

The establishment of one of the Centres for International Business Studies (CIBS) at Dalhousie University has contributed to the development of international course curriculum through research. The mandate of the CIBS is to foster teaching and research in international business and to provide outreach services to enhance Canada's competition in a global economy. Its primary objective is one of graduating a greater number of students with international business skills and knowledge. The Federal Department of External Affairs provides funding for the CIBS.

The Foreign Study Mission also adds to Dalhousie's international scope. Each year, nine first-year students go to Europe to work on special projects for their Canadian client company. For six to seven weeks the students, supervised by their academic adviser, research European technologies, make contacts, and/or collect data for the Canadian company they represent. They prepare a report for their client company and receive academic credit for their work. Although the timing of the Mission makes it difficult to get summer employment, the experience is invaluable. MacDougall describes the difference in the students who participated: "They left as students and acted as consultants over there."

# PART-TIME PROGRAM

■ SIZE OF INCOMING CLASS

40–45

Part-time students take classes alongside full-time students, and they can take courses either in the evening or during the day. Students have six years to complete their program, although the average is five.

Perhaps an area where Dalhousie falls short is the cost and flexibility of their part-time program. Initially, taking courses on a part-time basis can be expensive since the minimum charge of four courses is applied even though students may only register for one or two. However, tuition fees are capped at a figure equal to the full-time program.

When asked about Dalhousie's part-time program, Jamie Hannam, a current Dalhousie part-time student, describes the situation as one where "Dalhousie allows the part-time program more than promotes it." For example, students have six years to complete their program but Eileen MacDougall admits that "Unless students have advanced standing it would be difficult to complete the program in less than six years. Many students do the first year part-time and complete the second year full-time." Until September 1991, part-time students were not permitted to take more than four courses over a twelve-month period. This has been changed to permit students to take a fifth or sixth course during the summer term.

## PLACEMENT

Dalhousie has a Canada Employment Centre (CEC) that looks after placement for the entire university population. However, seventy-five per cent of the CEC's activity is accounted for by the MBA program. A placement officer — a paid position filled by students — complements the Canada Employment Centre. One student complained that there was not enough recruitment by companies from Ontario and the West, but that professors tried to help by putting you in touch with their contacts. A part-time student describes the effectiveness of the placement service as "I get calls from head-hunters at work but through Dal. nothing. A lot is put on the shoulders of the students themselves." Looking for a job requires job-search skills and an ability to focus on the career path you want. To help students in this area, Dalhousie offers a non-credit, compulsory course in career development. As one student mentions, "It doesn't just tell you about interviews and résumés but helps you find out what you want."

The top-three companies in terms of numbers of offers last year were

- Bank of Nova Scotia
- Royal Bank of Canada
- Export Development Corporation

## ON HALIFAX

Halifax has changed dramatically in the last ten years. The waterfront has been restored to a cobblestone, traffic-free, journey into yesteryear except that the old warehouses are now filled with interesting boutiques, sidewalk cafés, and restaurants.

It is a university town without equal in Canada. Halifax is the home of seven post-secondary institutions — Dalhousie University, King's College University, Mt. St. Vincent University, Nova Scotia Institute of Technology (NSIT), Nova Scotia School of Art and Design, St. Mary's University, and Technical University of Nova Scotia (TUNS). Dalhousie has a beautiful ivy-covered limestone campus within a twenty-minute walk of downtown and the waterfront. Although the campus is picturesque and full of history, the School of Business is a rabbit warren of narrow halls and windowless classrooms in a tired building. Only five minutes away is the St. Mary's campus.

Accommodation off-campus is hard to find. It is advisable to come to Halifax in July or August to "house hunt" because in September hardly anything is left. Six hundred dollars a month for a two-bedroom apartment is fairly cheap accommodation. The city of Halifax has a maritime atmosphere with a great night-life if you have the time and inclination.

## STUDENT PROFILES

*KAREN RADFORD*
MBA '91

- Full-time student in the MBA program
- Four-year BSc in Biology from Mount Allison University
- Entered her MBA right after undergraduate with no full-time work experience
- Her goal is to work in a multi-national corporation in investor relations with some connection to environmental issues
- Home town Riverview, New Brunswick
- Single

Karen had been accepted at York University as well as Dalhousie. She almost went to York but changed her mind at the last minute after calling up both schools and asking them why she should go there. Karen felt she got a more straightforward answer from Dalhousie.

One of the highlights of the MBA program for Karen was the Foreign Study Mission. Karen was one of nine students selected by the faculty and International Trade Canada to research expansion opportunities for Canadian-based companies abroad.

One month of domestic research was spent getting to know the companies' strengths, processes, and expectations. Also during this time, Karen attended workshops through the CIBC. Karen states, "I worked for a very technical company who was looking for a niche where they could expand before the barriers of the 1992 EEC came up."

The days were very full for Karen and the others since their mission was actually two-fold. They were working for their companies but they also toured various company plants including McCain, Volvo, and Northern Telecom.

Karen wrote a report explaining how they could adopt their technologies to the European market, identified the needs of the market, and named some key contacts. "A number of companies have followed up on the reports we presented," comments Karen.

"We decided that the Foreign Study Mission really tied in both the practical and theory we learned in the MBA. It was a great experience."


*PAUL RUDDERHAM*
MBA '90

- Part-time student in the MBA program
- Three-year BSc in Physics and Engineering from Mt. Allison University in 1982; four-year BSc Engineering from Technical University of Nova Scotia in 1984
- Worked throughout his MBA
- Worked for six years as an industrial engineer in Maritimes
- Currently employed as Communications Consultant in Sales and Marketing Department for Maritime Tel and Tel
- Home Town Sydney, Cape Breton
- Married, with two children

Paul chose Dalhousie because a number of his co-workers were taking their degree at Dalhousie, and "It has a good reputation for its academics."

He describes being a part-time student as, "There is no free time. Lunch times were not a break because you put down the pen, and start to prepare for a case." On the other hand, "You get more out of the part-time program because you only take one or two courses at a time, and therefore you get more focused. Full-time students are taking so many courses that they spread themselves too thin and don't get as much out of them. There is a monetary advantage to part-time. You don't give up a salary, and sometimes your company may sponsor you and pay all or most of your tuition." In Paul's case Maritime Tel and Tel paid seventy-five per cent of his tuition and books.

"The MBA has helped me. The learning process has helped me in my job, and it will help me in my career, but it doesn't guarantee me instant success."

# Ecole des Hautes Etudes Commerciales

- **INQUIRIES**

  Bureau de régistraire
  Ecole des Hautes Etudes Commerciales
  Université de Montréal
  5255 avenue Decelles
  Montréal, Québec
  H3T 1V6
  (514) 340-6136

## FULL-TIME PROGRAM

- **APPLICATION DEADLINE DATE FOR ADMISSIONS**

  | | |
  |---|---|
  | 1 April | Fall term |
  | 1 October | Winter term |

- **REQUIRED TO SUBMIT**
  - Two copies of official post-secondary transcripts
  - Three letters of recommendations
  - Personal statement and thirteen-page questionnaire
  - Résumé

- **AVERAGE GPA**

  3.3 or B+ or 76% (Minimum is 2.8 to 3.0 or B or 70–75%)
  3.5 or B+ or 80% is required for students with limited work experience

- **AVERAGE GMAT**

  GMAT scores are not required. However, Ecole des Hautes Etudes Commerciales has its own test, The Aptitude Test for Graduate Studies in Management, which Ecole des Hautes Etudes Commerciales requires applicants to write. The test is similar to the GMAT but it is in French and has been validated for their use. There is no minimum requirement on this test. GMAT scores are accepted if submitted and the candidate will not have to pass the Ecole des Hautes Etudes Commerciales test.

■ **PREFERENCE GIVEN TO A FOUR-YEAR DEGREE OVER A THREE-YEAR DEGREE?**
No
Twenty-five per cent of students in the class of 1990 have four-year degrees.

■ **NUMBER OF APPLICANTS**
573

■ **SIZE OF INCOMING CLASS**
54

■ **AVERAGE AGE OF STUDENTS**
29.5

■ **PERCENTAGE OF CLASS THAT ARE WOMEN**
40%

■ **PERCENTAGE OF CLASS WITH FULL-TIME WORK EXPERIENCE**
99%
The average length of full-time work experience is six to seven years
Two years relevant work experience is a requirement

■ **DISTRIBUTION OF UNDERGRADUATE DEGREES**

| | |
|---|---|
| BComm 27% | BA Humanities 8% |
| BSc Engineering 25% | Other Undergraduate 6% |
| BSc 15% | LLB 5% |
| BA Social Sciences 14% | |

■ **OTHER RELATED PROGRAMS**
Diploma in Administrative Studies and Master of Science in Management, PhD

Businesses are putting more emphasis on managers and executives possessing the so-called "soft skills" — such as good written and oral communication and interpersonal skills — and less on their ability to crank out numbers. The

Ecole des Hautes Etudes Commerciales at the Université de Montréal is responding to the needs of the business community. Ecole des Hautes Etudes Commerciales's program still has the same basic first-year program as other schools that introduce students to economics, financial and accounting principles, human resources management, management information systems, marketing, and organizational behaviour. However, it takes a qualitative approach by using a teaching style that is predominantly case. This gives an applied focus to the program. Simulations, applied practice, hands-on experience, presentations, and seminars are other teaching methods used.

Although it is a French program based in Canada's largest French-speaking city, it is not regionally based. Approximately twenty-four per cent of the student body comes from outside Quebec's francophone universities; twelve per cent comes from outside Canada, and another twelve per cent comes from anglophone universities.

Robert Desormeaux, MBA program Director, describes the student body at Ecole des Hautes Etudes Commerciales: "Our clientele are made up of people with good related work experience as well as high academic standing." He adds that "We have a mature but young clientele — young enough that an MBA can really make a difference in their career, but old enough that they can draw upon their experience." The program emphasizes the importance of students learning from each other.

The MBA program has a generalist focus but students can take four to six course concentrations in Finance, Human Resources, International Business, Management Information Systems, Marketing, Operations Management, or Small Businesses. Students can chose their electives from over sixty-three courses offered every year in their second year. For students who want a more theoretical approach to management, a Master of Science program is offered.

The establishment of one of the Centres for International Business Studies (CIBS) at Hautes des Ecoles Commerciales has contributed to the development of international course curriculum through its research. The mandate of the CIBS is to foster teaching and research in international business and to provide outreach services to enhance Canada's competition in a global economy. Its primary objective is one of graduating a greater number of students with international business skills and knowledge. The Federal Department of External Affairs provides funding for the CIBS.

Regarding tuition costs, although the tuition freeze of twenty years has been lifted, education in Quebec is still very reasonable when compared to the rest of Canada.

# PART-TIME PROGRAM

■ SIZE OF INCOMING CLASS
81

■ AVERAGE AGE OF STUDENTS
30

The same academic requirements stated for full-time students apply to part-time students also. Part-time students have a maximum of six years to complete their MBA, and the normal course load is one or two courses per semester. Transfers between part-time and full-time status are easily accommodated.

In recognition of fluctuating work loads at one's employment and unpredictable demands on one's personal life, students can go two semesters without taking courses. The academic year operates on a tri-semester system.

According to Robert Desormeaux, ninety per cent of the full-time students admitted finish the program as compared to fifty-five to sixty-five per cent of part-time students.

## PLACEMENT

Graduates of this general management program find employment in a wide range of employment sectors as the following statistics confirm. The average salary in 1990 was $54,000.

| | | | |
|---|---|---|---|
| Manufacturing | 28% | Services and Commerce | 11% |
| Financial | 18% | Energy and Utilities | 8% |
| Consulting | 13% | Government | 5% |
| Health and Education | 13% | Transportation | 4% |

At Ecole des Hautes Etudes Commerciales the placement function is in-house, but the great majority of students find their jobs on their own. Danièle Valiquette, MBA '91, who received her job offer through on-campus recruiting, describes the placement service as "very helpful. They do what they can but it's still up to the students."

The top recruiters through on-campus recruiting, in terms of numbers of offers given, were

• Bank of Canada     • National Bank     • Royal Bank of Canada

## ON MONTREAL

Ecole des Hautes Etudes Commerciales has one of the best business libraries in Canada. The campus is located five kilometres north of downtown Montreal. Housing is affordable and available close to campus. You do not have to live too close to the campus since the transit system is very good. It is advisable to use the transit since parking is a problem. The école's parking lots cost $150 a year or six dollars a day. There is little parking on the streets nearby, and parking tickets can cost thirty dollars.

One student comments that there was lots to do for entertainment, but it didn't make any difference since there was no time to enjoy it. Danièle Valiquette describes her "social life as greatly reduced. I socialize with the people at school but that's it. There is very little time off. Doing an MBA is like entering a convent."

## STUDENT PROFILES

### CHRISTIAN SAUVÉ
MBA '91

- Part-time student in the MBA program
- Four-year BSc Engineering (co-op) from the Université de Sherbrooke in 1983
- Works for Pratt & Whitney, an aircraft engines manufacturer, as an engineering supervisor
- Intends to continue working for Pratt & Whitney after graduation
- Home town Longueuil, Quebec, near Montreal
- Single

"I could have chosen McGill, or Concordia, but HEC was the oldest administration school in Montreal, and it had the best reputation," comments Christian.

The majority of courses are taught by the case method, and Christian considers this a "practical approach." Another applied component of the course that Christian values are the four or five projects where students have to act as consultants to a company. They study the problem and come up with recommendations to improve it.

"I did consider full-time but financially it was not feasible," mentions Christian. He adds that by going part-time he took classes with other part-time students at night, and he learned from their insights and enjoyed being with older people.

Christian credits the MBA for his promotion to supervisor. "It [the MBA] helped me get the promotion. Normally you don't get to be a supervisor when you are thirty years old." He also says he has a better understanding of the overall operation of the company. "I deal with people from manufacturing, purchasing, and customer support, and it's easier for me to find a solution now that will be good for everybody."


## DANIÈLE VALIQUETTE
MBA '91

- Part-time then full-time student in the MBA program
- Three-year BA in International Affairs from Concordia University in 1977
- Became a member of the Quebec Bar in 1982 after articling and completing a Civil Law Degree from the University of Ottawa
- Worked for the government for four years and then in the private sector for a family-run business as Vice President of Operations
- Hired as Director of Accounts for the National Bank in the corporate sector upon completion of MBA
- Home town Montreal

Danièle was in the unique situation of experiencing the MBA program both from a part-time and full-time perspective. In Danièle's opinion comparing part-time and full-time students was "like day and night." She describes the part-time experience as, "You go to your class and leave; you have less time to become integrated into the program and student life; priorities are divided between work and the MBA program." Danièle compares this to the full-time experience where "Our whole life is the MBA program; there is more competition and collegiality among the students."

Although Danièle concentrated in the finance area, she felt that the program focused on applying the principles and concepts rather than specializing on formulas and specifics. She explains that "The emphasis is put on developing your problem solving ability."

Another example of the applied nature of the program is that it is predominantly taught by the case method, even finance. In Danièle's opinion, "You were always put in contact with the real world . . . you learned to give practical real life solutions."

When asked where the program could improve, Danièle finds it difficult to criticize because she had enjoyed it so much. However, she comments that there was a lack of cases that were relevant to Quebec and that "Sometimes we see the same cases from semester to semester."

"I had some very high expectations when I entered the program, and they've all been met and more," Danièle states. She adds that "It's given me the tools that I will need . . . I don't believe you can be president overnight, but I believe what I've learned will give me the tools I can use."

# Laurentian University/ Université Laurentienne

- **INQUIRIES**

    Office of Admissions
    Laurentian University
    Ramsey Lake Road
    Sudbury, Ontario
    P3C 2C6
    (705) 675-1151 extension 3915

## PART-TIME PROGRAM

- **APPLICATION DEADLINE DATE FOR ADMISSIONS**

    31 May for September entry
    31 January for April admission
    The deadline may be extended until the quota of students is met.

- **REQUIRED TO SUBMIT**

    - GMAT score
    - Official post-secondary transcripts
    - TOEFL score is required from candidates whose first language is not English
    - Reference letters
    - Proof of two years full-time work experience

- **AVERAGE GPA**

    3.0 or B or 70%

- **AVERAGE GMAT**

    500
    If the GMAT is written more than once, the best score is used

- **PREFERENCE GIVEN TO A FOUR-YEAR DEGREE OVER A THREE-YEAR DEGREE?**

    No, unless there are more than thirty-five applicants

■ **SIZE OF INCOMING CLASS**
30 (35 is quota)

■ **PERCENTAGE OF CLASS WITH FULL-TIME WORK EXPERIENCE**
100%
Two years of full-time work experience is required

■ **OTHER RELATED PROGRAMS**
Graduate Diploma in Business

Laurentian University/Université Laurentienne is a bilingual university; however, the MBA program and other graduate-level course work is conducted in English. In 1960, Laurentian University/Université Laurentienne was created by an Act of the Ontario Parliament to meet the growing demand for university education in Northern Ontario. The MBA program serves the regional community who are already in the work force. It is primarily a part-time program with all courses offered in the evening and some required courses offered only in the Spring semester (April to July). The first year of the program can be taken on a full-time basis but, because resources are limited, it may not be possible for full-time students to complete the requirements within two years. Less than five full-time students are enrolled in the program this year.

The MBA program at Laurentian University/Université Laurentienne has a general management orientation, and students are not usually able to specialize in a particular subject area because of the small range of electives available at one time. However informal concentrations can be arranged, depending on the courses available, in Finance, Human Resources, and Marketing.

According to O. Ganjavi, Associate Professor and Director of the MBA program, the Faculty of Business Administration is trying to launch a formal concentration in Health Administration. Presently, the proposal is before the Ontario Council of Universities. If it is passed it will be implemented by September 1992.

Advanced standing is given to students who have taken equivalent courses in their undergraduate degrees. Students who have an honours degree in business administration, or an equivalent, may receive advanced standing in up to twelve of the twenty-two courses required, provided a mark of seventy per cent or better was obtained in each course. In special circumstances, mature students are admitted without an undergraduate degree. Candidates without an undergraduate degree are required to have a GMAT score at the seventy-five percentile rank or above and ten years of experience in business or the equivalent with evidence of achievement.

Enrolment in a minimum of one course each term, including intersession (summer term), is required and a maximum of eight years is allowed for the completion of the MBA program on a part-time basis. Students who have been given advanced standing will be required to complete the program in a shorter period of time computed on a pro-rata basis.

## PLACEMENT

The majority of the students enrolled in the MBA program at Laurentian University/Université Laurentienne are already employed. The Canada Employment Centre facilitates the job search for all Laurentian students.

## ON SUDBURY

The campus is located on the outskirts of Sudbury approximately twenty to twenty-five minutes from downtown by bus. It is set aside from the city of Sudbury and is situated between three lakes on 750 acres of land. The lakes provide excellent opportunities for swimming and sailing in the summer and skating and hockey in the winter. The campus backs onto a golf course, and down-hill and cross-country skiing and other sports are enjoyed throughout the year. Excellent physical education facilities are located on-campus. The buildings on-campus are poured concrete, giving a modern appearance. Most of the students live in the downtown area, but housing may be hard to find since the apartment vacancy rate is less than one per cent.

## STUDENT PROFILES

FRANK CATALANO
MBA '92

- Part-time student in the MBA program
- Four-year BSc in Mechanical Engineering from Queen's University in 1987
- Working for INCO as a first-line Supervisor
- INCO pays for Frank's MBA courses upon successful completion
- Hopes to get into upper management with INCO

- Home town Sudbury
- Married, and expecting their first child

In Frank's opinion, "They [the Faculty of Business Administration] have done their market research, and they know that their market is people in the work force." Therefore, the program is directed to the part-time student. Students enjoy a close relationship with the professors since the average class size is approximately fifteen, and, in Frank's opinion, this is a strength.

One concern of Frank's is that the Faculty "is trying to keep good quality professors but can't hold them."

Frank believes the MBA has helped him "enormously in terms of personal knowledge. It gives you the business background and people skills. It has given me a lot of tools and will give me a credential." On the other hand, Frank also perceives a negative effect of the MBA. "The downfall of the MBA is that it makes some people aggressive, competitive, and disloyal."


*SONIA DEL MISSIER*
MBA '91

- Part-time student in the MBA program
- Four-year Honours BSc in Languages from Laurentian University/ Université Laurentienne in 1978
- Has worked for Cambrian College for the past ten years, and her present position is Dean of Academic Support Programs Division
- Received support from the College for her MBA tuition of up to $400 a year through Staff Development and in terms of time off to study and work on assignments
- Intends to remain at Cambrian College for the short term
- Considering a PhD in business and other options such as foreign trade in the private sector
- Home town Sudbury
- Single

Sonia appreciates the fact that she can do her MBA in her home town of Sudbury and on a part-time basis. From working on her MBA since 1986, Sonia has a historical perspective of the program, and she is concerned about its future. "In 1986, the class sizes were big, and now the classes are smaller. I ask myself why. Are they limiting their base to Sudbury, and they have exhausted the market or is it because of limited courses not attracting students? I would hate to see the program die."

The small class size does provide an atmosphere that is less intimidating, and Sonia states, "I've never felt that I could not be open with my comments, including my concerns with the way the course would be taught."

Sonia also mentions that the professors are very accessible and would even give students their home telephone numbers. Sonia feels that this accessibility is important especially for part-time students since they are not there every day.

The MBA program has excellent professors in the areas of marketing and finance, in Sonia's opinion, but "They need full-time faculty. Right now they have quite a few part-time professors, and you never know if they are going to be there next year."

"Overall, I have enjoyed the experience. I have learned a lot, and I feel confident that I could go out and look for a job in marketing . . . I think there is a lot of potential for the MBA program at Laurentian," concludes Sonia.

# Université Laval

---

■ **INQUIRIES**

Directeur des programmes MBA et DA
Pavilion des sciences de l'administration
Université Laval
Ste-Foy, Québec
GIK 7P4
(418) 656-3521

## FULL-TIME PROGRAM

■ **APPLICATION DEADLINE DATE FOR ADMISSIONS**

31 May

■ **REQUIRED TO SUBMIT**

• Reference letters
• Personal statements
• Résumé

■ **AVERAGE GPA**

MBA Plan A   3.5 or B+ or 78%
MBA Plan B   3.5 or B+ or 78%

■ **PREFERENCE GIVEN TO A FOUR-YEAR DEGREE OVER A THREE-YEAR DEGREE?**

Yes

■ **NUMBER OF APPLICANTS**

MBA Plan A   183 (includes part-time)
MBA Plan B   258 (includes part-time)

■ **SIZE OF INCOMING CLASS**

MBA Plan A   57 (only full-time)
MBA Plan B   133 (only full-time)

- **AVERAGE AGE OF STUDENTS**

  MBA Plan A and MBA Plan B combined   29

- **PERCENTAGE OF CLASS THAT ARE WOMEN**

  MBA Plan A   41%
  MBA Plan B   33%

- **PERCENTAGE OF CLASS WITH FULL-TIME WORK EXPERIENCE**

  MBA Plan A   100%
  Applicants are required to have at least two years experience in administration, but average is four or five years
  MBA Plan B   less than 10% of the student body have work experience

- **DISTRIBUTION OF UNDERGRADUATE DEGREES**

  Students in the MBA Plan A program come from agriculture, arts, educational science, engineering, food sciences, forestry, law, medical sciences, pharmacy, psychology, pure sciences, and social sciences to name a few. Precise statistics are not available.

  The MBA Plan B student body is made up predominantly of students with a Bachelor of Commerce degree or some other degree pertinent to what they want to specialize in, for example, Actuarial Sciences for Finance, Computer Sciences for Management Information Systems, Industrial Engineering for Operation Decision Making, Industrial Relations or Psychology for Management. Precise statistics are not available.

- **OTHER RELATED PROGRAMS**

  Diploma in Administration, Diploma of Administrative Studies, Master of Health Administration, Master of Industrial Relations, Master of Public Administration, and PhD

Instruction at Université Laval's MBA Program is in French, but a mastery of at least written English is required since the majority of written information, including textbooks, is in English.

Two MBA programs are offered at Université Laval. The first, Plan A, is a generalist MBA offered to applicants with a wide variety of undergraduate backgrounds. The second, Plan B, is a specialized program most appropriate for applicants with a Bachelor of Commerce background who want to concentrate in Accounting, Applied Economics, Finance, International Business, Management, Management Information Systems, Marketing,

Operation Decision Making. The administration is currently in the process of changing the Plan B MBA program to a Master of Science, which would be more reflective of its specialized nature.

Gerard Verna, Director of the MBA program, describes Université Laval's niche: "We take the humanist approach, where people are more important than money. We call it the 'Laval style.' " The emphasis on the individual starts during the admission process for the Plan A program where each candidate is interviewed. "We are looking for people who have a very active life. We concentrate more on their work experience than their academic standing past the minimum requirements," comments Verna. Candidates for the Plan B program do not require an interview. Most of the emphasis is placed on academic performance rather than work experience.

Also important is an applicant's competency in math and statistics. A university-level course in each of these subjects is a pre-requisite of admission to the program. Candidates who do not have this background can be granted conditional admission subject to the successful completion of a math and statistics remedial course offered during the summer preceding the commencement of classes in September.

In the generalist program, Plan A, there are no concentrations in the functional areas, but students can focus on specific sectors, for example, international or social services. A three-month summer work-term in an international corporation or a social services setting such as a hospital is required. This work-term is arranged by the student. It is not a co-op arrangement.

An exchange program with York University helps students to become more familiar with English language and culture. The percentage of students from outside Québec and abroad is up to forty-five per cent in the MBA Plan B program. In the Plan A program, approximately ten per cent are from outside Québec.

Université Laval has been very involved in MBA competitions and has placed second and third in 1990 and 1989, respectively, in the Concordia MBA Case Competition and third in 1990 in the Royal Bank Business Student Writing Awards.


## PART-TIME PROGRAM

■ SIZE OF INCOMING CLASS
    MBA Plan A   40
    MBA Plan B   65

Students enrolled in the part-time program at Laval have four years to complete the requirements of the program. Courses are offered both during the day and evening, but most students take the majority of their classes during the day. Each semester, three or four courses are offered during the evening or on week-ends. Registration in a minimum of two courses per year is required.

## PLACEMENT

Job search support is available through the Canada Employment Centre (CEC) on-campus. The CEC services the entire Laval student population.

The top-five companies in terms of numbers of offers last year were

- Procter & Gamble
- Banque Royale du Canada
- Hydro Québec
- Canadien Pacifique
- Arthur Andersen Conseil

## ON STE-FOY

The first buildings of Université Laval's campus were built in the 1950s, creating an architecturally modern campus that is approximately twenty minutes from "old" Quebec by bus. The MBA program is housed in a brand new building, finished in 1990, the De Seve Pavillon. Some buildings and residences are connected by a network of underground tunnels.

## STUDENT PROFILES

*JEAN-PAUL CARRIER*
MBA '91

- Part-time student in Plan A of the MBA program
- Three-year Licence en Lettres in Modern Languages from Université Laval in 1968
- Worked for eighteen years as a foreign service officer until he left in 1986, when he became chief of staff to Quebec's Minister of International and Intergovernmental Affairs and started his MBA at Université Laval
- Presently owns his own consulting firm dealing with international affairs
- Intends on continuing in consulting and building his business

- Home town Matane, Quebec, approximately 400 km outside of Québec City
- Married, with three children

"Everyone wants to learn a little more. I was forty-two years old when I started my MBA, and I thought that going back to university was a good way to learn new ideas. I thought it would open new doors," comments Jean-Paul.

Initially Jean-Paul started his MBA at the University of Ottawa, and when he was transferred to New York he continued his studies at New York State University. Université Laval accepted most of his transfer credits.

"I have noticed a trend that Laval is focusing its efforts on the day students, favouring full concentration on their studies," Jean-Paul states. He adds that it was relatively easy to complete the first year of the MBA by taking evening courses, but that it got increasingly difficult past that level. However, Jean-Paul felt that this was partly compensated for by the courses offered through intensive weekend sessions.

In Jean-Paul's opinion, Université Laval offers a good general MBA with an emphasis on the practical aspects of management. An example of this was an international marketing study Jean-Paul conducted with a small Canadian enterprise who wanted to export to the United States. Jean-Paul adds that, "Students participate and do a lot of presentations in class." Jean-Paul appreciated the fact that a number of professors came from the business sector.

The MBA has helped Jean-Paul. "The MBA program at Laval teaches students good work methods. It was very refreshing for me to talk to professors and other younger students. The theory opened up new perspectives for me," concludes Jean-Paul.


*LOUISE JONCAFF*
MBA '91

- Full-time student in Plan A of the MBA program
- Three-year BA in Industrial Relations from Université Laval in 1987
- Worked as a personnel director in small businesses
- Wants to continue in personnel but with a large corporation
- Home town Québec City
- Married, with two children

"Having managerial work experience is very important," Louise comments. In Louise's class, students had from two to more than ten years of related work experience, and this made the discussions more interesting and applicable.

When asked what the main strength of the program was, Louise answers that "The theoretical content was there, but there was also a lot of practical exercises that we did outside of the university with businesses. For me, the practical activities were very important."

Laval has introduced a new approach to teaching by using modules. These intensive integrative sessions occur throughout the year and could be from one to three weeks in length depending on the topic. For example, Management or Marketing were taught in this way.

The module approach of teaching was a strength, but it was sometimes a disadvantage too, in Louise's opinion. In accounting, Louise felt that the traditional approach would be a better teaching method than the use of modules. "Accounting only has thirty hours of class time which isn't sufficient. It only gives a basic understanding of the subject," states Louise. "Perhaps we need both the traditional and the module approach for these areas," suggests Louise.

Louise has benefitted from the MBA program at Laval. "It has helped me to know myself better and to develop some abilities and attitudes. I have developed a more global vision."

# University of Manitoba

- **INQUIRIES**
  MBA Program
  Faculty of Management
  University of Manitoba
  Winnipeg, Manitoba
  R3T 2N2
  (204) 474-8448

## FULL-TIME PROGRAM

- **APPLICATION DEADLINE DATE FOR ADMISSIONS**
  May 1

- **REQUIRED TO SUBMIT**
  - GMAT score
  - Official post-secondary transcripts
  - TOEFL score is required from candidates whose first language is not English
  - Reference letters
  - Personal statement
  - Résumé
  - MBA program supplementary application form

- **AVERAGE GPA**
  3.4 or B+ or 78%

- **AVERAGE GMAT**
  590–600
  If the GMAT is written more than once, the best score is used

- **PREFERENCE GIVEN TO A FOUR-YEAR DEGREE OVER A THREE-YEAR DEGREE?**
  Yes, but both are considered

- **NUMBER OF APPLICANTS**

  208

- **SIZE OF INCOMING CLASS**

  39

- **AVERAGE AGE OF STUDENTS**

  28

- **PERCENTAGE OF CLASS THAT ARE WOMEN**

  34%

- **PERCENTAGE OF CLASS WITH FULL-TIME WORK EXPERIENCE**

  91% (Average length of work experience is five years)

- **DISTRIBUTION OF UNDERGRADUATE DEGREES**

  | BA 30% | Other Undergraduate 12% |
  |---|---|
  | BSc 25% | BComm 9% |
  | BSc Engineering 18% | BSc Agriculture 6% |

- **OTHER RELATED PROGRAMS**

  Master of Accounting, Master of Actuarial Science, and Master of Operations Research

In 1988, the University of Manitoba made a decision radical from the mainstream. The administration appointed a dean from the private sector rather than from academia to head their Faculty of Management. William Mackness was the senior vice-president with the Bank of Nova Scotia prior to appointment at the University of Manitoba. His area of expertise in the banking community was economic forecasting, and he is a graduate of the University of Western Ontario, where he received his masters in economics.

"Dean Mackness brings a fresh outlook and is committed to raising the profile and standards of the school. The Dean's philosophy is that this [the MBA program] is a flagship program for the school of business," comments Susan Eide, MBA Program Manager. His strength lies in his abilities to develop strategic plans for organizational change and development.

Student needs are one of Dean Mackness's top priorities. He was tested on his commitment when a group of students requested that the business building remain open later in the evening. The building housed library and computing facilities that fell outside the jurisdiction of the Faculty of Management but Dean Mackness worked with all concerned to satisfy the request of the students. David Brickwood, MBA '91, describes Dean Mackness: "He has a vision of what he wants the school to be." The Dean occasionally gives lectures, which allows the students to see his views. The Associate Dean also teaches within the program and knows the students by name. Direction of the program is partly guided by the Associate Program. Approximately 250 prominent business people from Winnipeg and across Canada (chapters in Toronto and Vancouver), support the school and act in an advisory capacity. Their input keeps the school well informed of the skills and preparation expected of MBA graduates by the business community.

To finance new initiatives, and the proposed PhD program, Dean Mackness introduced a Faculty Development Plan. This plan proposed a major infusion of funding to be provided by the students, the associates, the university, and the provincial government. In a referendum, the students approved a tuition surcharge, which provided the leverage for the other funding sources. By 1995 the Development Plan will increase the Faculty's budget by approximately thirty per cent.

The MBA program at the University of Manitoba is a mainstream general management program. Susan Eide states, "It is what MBA schools were first designed to be." The curriculum is reviewed every year to keep it up to date. In second year, students can choose up to four courses in accounting, agribusiness, finance, generalist, marketing, personnel, public policy, or quantitative methods to form a concentration. The agribusiness concentration was introduced three years ago and is unique to the University of Manitoba. Fifty per cent of students choose the generalist management option.

The University of Manitoba is primarily a regional university that maintains a graduate-level business program for central Canada. Approximately seventy per cent of the student enrolment in the MBA program comes from the province of Manitoba. The program is small with an incoming full-time class of forty. The faculty pride themselves on the personalized treatment that students receive. In Susan Eide's opinion, the personalized treatment begins during the admission process. Each candidate's file is looked at closely. Susan particularly looks at whether part-time applicants have just received a promotion, have heavy travel commitments, or have an extreme work commitment. Susan asks herself, "Is this person ready for this program at this time?" References are checked, and they have been known to phone an applicant if something is ambiguous or if more detail is needed. University-level math courses in calculus and algebra are strongly recommended as part of the admission requirements. Applicants may be admitted without these if they can demonstrate a quantitative aptitude through their GMAT or work experience. A non-credit math course in the first term of the MBA program will be required of students lacking calculus and algebra.

## PART-TIME PROGRAM

■ **NUMBER OF APPLICANTS**
95

■ **SIZE OF INCOMING CLASS**
41

■ **AVERAGE AGE OF STUDENTS**
30

Part-time students have a maximum of six years to complete the MBA program at the University of Manitoba, and a minimum course load of at least two courses per regular session is required. Students have the option of taking classes during the day or evening and are mixed with the full-time students.

## PLACEMENT

Placement is handled both through the Canada Employment Centre, which is responsible for the entire university, and through the Faculty of Management, which employs its own in-house placement co-ordinator. The in-house placement service is only one year old and was partly funded by the Development Plan. The placement service and the MBA and Commerce programs are all housed within the Drake Building.

A list of the top companies in terms of numbers of offers last year is not available.

## ON WINNIPEG

The University of Manitoba's campus is located in the southern part, on the outskirts of the city of Winnipeg. Most of the MBA students have a car, but the bus system is good. By car, the downtown core is approximately fifteen to twenty minutes away, and by bus it takes thirty minutes. One student suggested that, if you own a car, it is advisable to apply for parking in April since you are competing with undergraduates for parking space. The Faculty of Management is housed in the Drake Building which is only five years old. The MBA students have their own wing within the building and a student lounge dedicated to MBA's. David Brickwood, MBA '91, describes the atmosphere of the city as, "a little bit cliquey since the people have been here forever. They're not moving all the time like in Toronto." He adds that "The bonding is very good, however, among the MBA students."

Housing is available and very cheap. A new one-bedroom apartment can go for around four hundred dollars and older ones for three hundred dollars easily. Food and entertainment are also cheaper than in the more major cities of Toronto, Montreal, and Vancouver.

Dress warmly because Winnipeg is known for its cold temperatures. But take heart, the skies are mostly sunny, and springs are gorgeous starting about April, when classes end.

## STUDENT PROFILES

*IRÈNE CROWE*
MBA '91

- Part-time student for one year, then switched to full-time student in the MBA program
- Four-year BSc in Biochemistry/Genetics from McGill University in 1967; RN from the Health Science Centre in Winnipeg
- Worked for a few years in labs both at McGill and Dalhousie
- Took the next ten years off to be a full-time mother
- Worked in a hospital for four years, and as a VON for two years
- Short-term goal targeting labour relations in the non-profit sector
- Eventually wants to own her own business
- Home town Montreal
- Single parent, with two children

Irène began the MBA program part-time while working as a VON. However, after a year she quit her job and attended school full-time. "Having a family and being a single parent, I found it too much trying to study, work, and look after my family."

Last summer Irène acted as a consultant to small businesses in the Winnipeg community. Irène was one of ten students hired as part of the MBA Summer Student Consulting Program. The program is funded by the Faculty of Management and the Provincial Government.

In Irène's opinion, the Business school has close ties with the business community. Speakers are brought in, and members from the business community are sometimes involved in the classes. For example, in Irène's second-year collective bargaining course, one of their assignments was an arbitration hearing case they presented to the head of the Labour Board to adjudicate. Another project in the course was to negotiate a collective agreement. The group was divided into union and management. Teamsters and management from the community were brought in as advisors. They also evaluated the group along with a third party from the government.

The professor of the collective bargaining course was Gary Nuttal. To Irène, he was one of the best professors she had ever had. "He taught us listening skills and made us aware of how much body language, seating arrangements, and the colour a person chose to wear could tell us." Another excellent professor, Irène recalls, is Ross Henderson who teaches first-year production and second-year policy. "He is a man of integrity and fairness. He pushes us to be professional and thorough, and brought out the best in me."

When asked where the MBA program could improve, Irène comments that the curriculum did not include a course on ethics. "It is touched on briefly in other courses, but I think it should be a separate course — and compulsory."

By taking the MBA at the University of Manitoba, "I have gained personal growth, presentation skills, confidence in front of groups, and confidence over-all. It also gave me business skills that were completely foreign to me prior to the program. I expect it will open doors for me."


*BRUCE HICKS*
MBA '93

- Part-time student in the MBA program
- Four-year BSc in Engineering Surveying from the University of New Brunswick in 1980; MSc in Surveying from the University of New Brunswick in 1987
- Works with the Manitoba provincial government as an engineer in the survey and mapping department
- Employer (provincial government) sponsors him in the MBA program by paying for fifty per cent of his tuition and books
- Home town Kenora, Ontario
- Married, with four children

If it had been financially possible, Bruce would have enrolled in the MBA program as a full-time student. "First year doesn't matter since the courses stand alone and are technical. But in second year how strongly can you link things together when it is stretched out over two or three years?" He adds that it would have been difficult to do the program without the support of his wife. "She gives me moral support and sometimes a good swift kick to get me going."

Bruce comments on the good relationship between the students and faculty and the small size of the program. The average size of a first-year required course is approximately thirty-five whereas in second year some elective courses can have as few as fifteen.

The atmosphere at the University of Manitoba was like a day-school in Bruce's opinion. "The majority of students are from the town [of Winnipeg]. The university population goes to school during the day and home at night." Approximately seventy per cent of the students attending the program are from Manitoba.

Has taking the MBA helped Bruce? "I have moved out of the technical area and into management, and the skills that I am learning are applicable."

# McGill University

■ **INQUIRIES**

The McGill MBA Program
Faculty of Management
Samuel Bronfman Building
McGill University
1001 rue Sherbrooke Ouest
Montréal, Québec
H3A 1G5
(514) 398-3876

## FULL-TIME PROGRAM

■ **APPLICATION DEADLINE DATE FOR ADMISSIONS**

1 June
15 March recommended deadline for international students

■ **REQUIRED TO SUBMIT**

- GMAT score
- Official post-secondary transcripts
- Reference letters
- Personal statement
- Résumé

■ **AVERAGE GPA**

3.2 or B+ or 75% (with emphasis on a positive progression in grades with the last year weighted the most)

■ **AVERAGE GMAT**

Approximately 600
If the GMAT is written more than once, the best score is used

- **PREFERENCE GIVEN TO A FOUR-YEAR DEGREE OVER A THREE-YEAR DEGREE**

  No

- **NUMBER OF APPLICANTS**

  900

- **SIZE OF INCOMING CLASS**

  120

- **AVERAGE AGE OF STUDENTS**

  25

- **PERCENTAGE OF CLASS THAT ARE WOMEN**

  35%

- **PERCENTAGE OF CLASS WITH FULL-TIME WORK EXPERIENCE**

  75% (Average length of work experience is two years)

- **DISTRIBUTION OF UNDERGRADUATE DEGREES**

  | | |
  |---|---|
  | BSc 38% | BSc Engineering 12% |
  | BA 30% | Other Undergraduate 2% |
  | BComm/BBA 18% | |

- **OTHER RELATED PROGRAMS**

  MBA/Diploma in Management (Asian Studies) and MBA/LAW

The McGill administration prides itself on the quality of their students. According to W.B. Crowston, Dean of the Faculty of Management, "We take cutoffs very seriously on the GMAT and GPA." Students with marginal standing may be interviewed, and for these students reference letters can be especially important. In Dean Crowston's opinion, the best referees know the student well enough to be able to give specific examples of his or her leadership abilities or other strengths.

It is possible to enter McGill's MBA program with no full-time work experience. In fact, twenty-five per cent of the students enrolled in the program do not have full-time work experience. Involvement in student government, internships, experience in starting your own small business, or experience abroad are regarded favourably.

Although math is not a pre-requisite, a package of material reviewing the expectations in the areas of math and stats is sent to every student offered admission. Proficiency in these areas is expected as well as computer proficiency in WordPerfect and Lotus.

Education in Montreal benefits from low tuition. Although the twenty-year freeze on tuition has been lifted, fees are still significantly lower than at other universities outside Quebec.

McGill's MBA program has an international orientation. In the McGill calendar, Dean Crowston states, "We have chosen to become the leader in international management education." An international orientation is expressed by the high percentage and mixture of foreign students enrolled in McGill's MBA. Forty per cent of this year's class are foreign students with twenty-three different countries represented. The first students from Thailand and Japan attended McGill this year.

The faculty at McGill can claim national origin in more than a dozen countries. Their interests and outlooks are international, and a number have proven themselves to be in the forefront of research in cross-cultural and multinational business issues.

Exchange programs have been arranged with France, Spain, England, Sweden, Germany, Belgium, Italy, and the United States. Twenty students in second year spend one or two semesters abroad, and McGill acts as a host to over twenty students from other countries.

McGill is the only Canadian member of the Program in International Management (PIM), a consortium of institutions offering graduate-level degrees. McGill is also involved in the Canada-China Project. McGill and nine other Canadian universities are helping the People's Republic of China train future managers in the business and public sector. The McGill calendar describes the project as benefitting McGill MBA students, who gain exposure and insight into China's rapidly developing economy.

## PART-TIME PROGRAM

■ **NUMBER OF APPLICANTS**
600

■ **SIZE OF INCOMING CLASS**
150 (700 part-time students at McGill)

Students pay per course, and they are not required to maintain any mandatory minimum course load. It is an open program in which students can move through at their own pace. All part-time courses are offered in the evening.

A selection of second-year day courses are also available to part-time students. Also, students have the option to transfer to second year on a full-time basis after completing the first year part-time. The maximum time limit to complete the part-time program is six years.


## PLACEMENT


The MBA program has its own placement officer who offers workshops on interviewing and résumés and facilitates on-campus recruiting. Graduating students can also include their résumé in the *Graduating Class*, a book that is sent to major employers in Canada and selected employers in the United States and Europe. Over eighty firms recruit at McGill.

Top-five companies in terms of numbers of offers last year were

- American Express
- Procter & Gamble
- Warner Lambert
- Northern Telecom Inc.
- Royal Bank of Canada


## ON MONTREAL


McGill is in the heart of Montreal and a few minutes walk from Concordia University. McGill's Faculty of Management is housed in the Samuel Bronfman Building on Sherbrooke Street West. On Boulevard St.-Laurent, a ten-minute walk from the university, you can dine inexpensively in small European restaurants inviting you to savour German, Portuguese, or Italian dishes. A little further south is Montreal's Chinese community. If the establishments are not licensed it is quite legal to bring your own alcoholic beverages. Montreal has a European flavour at North American prices.

Bring warm clothing because Montreal is bitterly cold in the winter. To entice shoppers, in such cold temperatures, an excellent underground system of corridors link individual buildings to each other and to the Metro subway downtown core.

Housing is very easy to come by. One student told a story about how his friend from Iceland arrived four days before classes started and got an apartment within an eight-minute walk from campus and within his price range with no problem at all. Prices are relatively inexpensive.

One student commented, "It was heartbreaking. So much fun available but so much work to do."

# STUDENT PROFILES

*ELIZABETH BALDWIN-JONES*
MBA '91

- Full-time student in the MBA program
- Three-year BA in History/Political Science from McGill University in 1989
- Targeting government job in external affairs or an international department/government relations division in the public or private sector
- Home town Ottawa
- Single

In keeping with Elizabeth's goal to work in External Affairs, she was attracted to McGill's MBA program because of the emphasis on international studies.

Not having work experience, she thought her chances would be better at McGill because she knew that McGill accepted students straight out of undergraduate studies. If she had been rejected, she was going to get some work experience before reapplying.

At first Elizabeth was a little concerned about taking her masters degree at the same institution that she obtained her undergraduate degree. However, "The MBA was very different from my undergraduate degree so I didn't feel I was getting the same approach."

Along with many other students in the MBA program, Elizabeth comments on the high quality of teaching: Jay Conger in Organizational Behaviour had "excellent presentations," and Jan Jorgensen in Policy and Public Sector Management was "very knowledgeable."

Another strength of the program in Elizabeth's opinion was the second-year core-policy course. "The emphasis was on group projects directly involving hands-on experience with a company. This was especially important to me because I didn't have work experience."

On the down side, Elizabeth was frustrated by courses that were listed in the calendar but not offered.

Elizabeth is confident that she made the right decision in taking an MBA. "I always knew I was going to graduate school. I thought of Law, but I thought the MBA would be more portable. It's a practical degree [that] makes me trainable. I have the basics and can pick things up quickly."

*MICHAEL GARLICK*
MBA '92

- Full-time student in the MBA program
- BSc in Electrical Engineering from GMI Engineering and Management Institute in Flint, Michigan, in 1987
- Worked for General Motors
- Wants to stay in a manufacturing or industrial setting
- Home town Glencoe, Ontario, near London
- Married

Both Michael and his wife are enrolled in McGill's MBA program. After graduation, they hope to work in the States.

Michael chose McGill because the school had recognition with Americans he had worked with. He had considered applying to an American MBA program but it was not financially feasible, and they were attracted to living in downtown Montreal.

Next year, Michael hopes to be selected to take part in the international exchange program. Students take their second term of their final year in another country.

The international emphasis is also felt in the student mixture at McGill. Michael comments that in his classes there were people from Turkey, the United States, Japan, China, and Australia and that they brought unique perspectives to the discussions.

Michael was quite impressed with the professors at McGill — especially Jay Conger, an Organizational Behaviour professor. He comments that, even though there were seventy students in the class, Professor Conger was "really energetic" and brought a lot of experience into the classroom.

Coming from an engineering background, Michael felt that he needed the background provided by the compulsory basic first-year courses. However, he mentions that some of his friends with commerce backgrounds and little work experience were discontented.

Michael has one piece of advice that he would like to pass on to perspective MBAs. "I would recommend at least two year's work experience. There were certain examples in class that we [students with work experience] could understand and remember happening to us. People who only worked for a few months during the summer didn't get the same out of it."

# McMaster University

- **INQUIRIES**

    Administrator
    MBA Program
    Faculty of Business
    Kenneth Taylor Hall
    Room 118
    McMaster University
    Hamilton, Ontario
    L8S 4M4
    (416) 525-9140 extension 4433

## FULL-TIME PROGRAM

- **APPLICATION DEADLINE DATE FOR ADMISSIONS**

    15 July subject to availability of places
    1 June for Visa applicants

- **REQUIRED TO SUBMIT**
    - GMAT score
    - Official post-secondary transcripts
    - TOEFL score is required from candidates whose first language is not English
    - Reference letters
    - Personal statement recommended
    - Résumé recommended

- **AVERAGE GPA**

    8.8 on a 12-point scale or B+ or 78%

- **AVERAGE GMAT**

    613

The March sitting of the GMAT is recommended
If the GMAT is written more than once, the most recent score is used

- **PREFERENCE GIVEN TO A FOUR-YEAR DEGREE OVER A THREE-YEAR DEGREE?**

    No

- **NUMBER OF APPLICANTS**

    303

- **SIZE OF INCOMING CLASS**

    68

- **AVERAGE AGE OF STUDENTS**

    25

- **PERCENTAGE OF CLASS THAT ARE WOMEN**

    38%

- **DISTRIBUTION OF UNDERGRADUATE DEGREES**

    | | |
    |---|---|
    | BSc 43% | Engineering 7% |
    | BA Social Science 28% | Humanities 5% |
    | BBA/BComm 13% | Other 4% including Law and applicants without an undergraduate degree |

- **OTHER RELATED PROGRAMS**

    PhD in Human Resources and Labour Relations, PhD in Management Science/Systems

McMaster's MBA program has a general management focus, but it is possible to concentrate through highly structured streams. Specific core courses are set down within each stream, and students must declare their area of concentration before beginning the final ten courses in the program. Students can choose from the following streams: Accounting, Finance, General MBA, Health Services Management (only offered through Co-op or part-time), Human Resources and Labour Relations, Information Systems, International Business, Logistics/Production/Operations, Management Science, and Marketing.

On the continuum of qualitative versus quantitative, McMaster's MBA program definitely falls toward the quantitative end of the scale. Gary Waterfield, Director of Graduate Admissions and Students Affairs, states that applicants must demonstrate their proficiency in math by having undergraduate courses in calculus and linear algebra within the last five years, or by writing waiver exams. Applicants who are judged weak in this area may be granted provisional admission. The McMaster calendar makes it quite clear that, "It is strongly recommended that students on provisional admission clear the mathematics requirement before starting their first term by successful completion of introductory calculus and linear algebra courses approved by the Faculty of Business."

Computing skills are an integral part of the MBA Program at McMaster. Upon admission, students receive a letter from the chairman of the advisory committee with a list of expectations, states Gary Waterfield.

Unique to McMaster is the Japan Study Program. The program gives students the opportunity to take courses in Japan for credit toward their MBA at McMaster. Each year, a limited number of students (four in February 1991), study at the Institute for International Studies and Training (IIST) located on the slopes of Mount Fuji during the February to May period. The McMaster calendar describes it as "Together with some forty MBA's from one French and seven US universities, our students study, socialize, and live with trainees from major Japanese companies. In addition to taking courses selected from a variety of international business subjects, students study the Japanese language and topics dealing specifically with Japanese business, government, and culture."

To be eligible to participate in the Japan Study Program, students must have a GPA of 6.0 or more, the specified international business course, and successful completion of a Japanese language course. Courses in Japanese language are offered at McMaster University, Sheridan College in Mississauga, and Humber College in Toronto.

In December of 1991 the Faculty of Business will be moving to its new facility — the Michael DeGroote School of Business Building named after Michael DeGroote, President and Chief Executive Officer of Laidlaw Transportation Ltd. DeGroote plays an active role on McMaster's Business Advisory Council established in 1972. The stated goal of the Council is to "contribute to the recognition and advancement of the McMaster University Faculty of Business as one of Canada's leading business schools." McMaster's link with the business community was key to the construction of the new Michael DeGroote School of Business Building. Funds for the new Business building came completely from the private sector, with no government contribution.

# CO-OP PROGRAM

- **REQUIRED TO SUBMIT**
  Résumé required in addition to items listed under full-time program

- **NUMBER OF APPLICANTS**
  146

- **SIZE OF INCOMING CLASS**
  53

- **AVERAGE AGE OF STUDENTS**
  25

"Innovation in Education" is part of McMaster University's motto. Within the MBA program this innovation comes through in their Co-op Program. McMaster is one of three universities in Canada that offer an MBA Co-op Program. Founded in 1971, the Co-op MBA brochure describes it as "North America's largest MBA Co-op program." Regarding work terms, the brochure goes on to say, "Our students work in both large and small companies, hospitals, and governments in Ontario, Quebec, Alberta, British Columbia, the United States, in Europe, and the Far East."

The advantage of the Co-op program is that it allows students to put into practice what they are learning in their work-terms. This integration of knowledge and practice takes on a very applied and broad-based approach. Susan Martin, Manager of the MBA Co-op program and Placement Service, comments that the Co-op program is particularly good for "students with either no work experience or two to five years with unrelated work experience. It is a great opportunity to test out what you really want. Until you are working in the environment, you are still dealing with perceptions and expectations."

Susan Martin also comments that another advantage to Co-op is that it gives students a chance to mature and "allows for the MBA syndrome to be defused." This syndrome can be described as an attitude of "Here I am." In her opinion, co-op students are more realistic than some full-time MBA students, especially those with little work experience."

The Co-op program alternates four-month periods of study and work throughout the program, which is twenty-eight months in length. This alternating schedule give students an opportunity to get a year-round experience exposing them to most aspects of an organization's yearly cycle.

The McMaster calendar states that, "Work positions are available in chartered accountancy, institutional management (government, hospitals, etc.), private industry, and financial institutions. In scope, a wide variety of jobs are offered which encompass many of the functional areas of business. However, students should not anticipate working in a supervisory or managerial capacity." Richard Kung, MBA '92, comments on the availability of work-terms during the recession — "The administration doesn't guarantee you a position but in this time of recession I am not aware of anyone who didn't get a work placement." Susan Martin confirms this and comments that "The last time there was a student not placed was in 1982."

To gain admission into the Co-op program, applicants must first meet the qualifications for the full-time program. In addition, they must possess Canadian citizenship or landed-immigrant status with at least one year's residency in Canada. If the applicant satisfies the basic admission requirements, they are offered an interview by the Faculty of Business for a place in the Co-op program. According to Susan Martin, flexibility is one factor that is checked during the interview since the Co-op program, perhaps even more so than the full-time program, is very structured. The interview process is designed to be a two-way communication. If a candidate is unsuccessful, they will automatically be offered a place in the full-time or part-time program.

The Co-op program can only be taken on a full-time basis, and no advance standing is given. Course exemptions for up to five courses may be allowed if a student has taken equivalent courses. Only through the Co-op and part-time programs can students take the Health Services Management Stream. Other streams that are available are Accounting, Finance, General Management, Human Resources and Labour Relations, Information Systems, International Business, Logistics/Production/Operations, Management Science, and Marketing.

## PART-TIME PROGRAM

■ **NUMBER OF APPLICANTS**
136

■ **SIZE OF INCOMING CLASS**
68

■ **AVERAGE AGE OF STUDENTS**
30

- **PERCENTAGE OF CLASS THAT ARE WOMEN**
  27%

- **DISTRIBUTION OF UNDERGRADUATE DEGREES**

  | | |
  |---|---|
  | BSc Engineering 40% | BA Social Science 10% |
  | BSc 23% | BA Humanities 3% |
  | BBA/BComm 16% | Other Undergraduate 8% |

Part-time students may register in a maximum of two courses in each session. On this basis, a part-time student can complete the full program in a minimum of just over three years or in less time if advanced standing is granted on admission. The maximum time limit is eight years. This would be pro-rated if advanced standing was given on admission. Students cannot miss more than two consecutive terms. Evening courses are held on week days (Monday through Thursday) during the period 7–10 p.m. and, in limited cases, on Saturday morning; i.e., one three-hour session per week per course.

The admission requirements, curriculum, and expected standards of performance are the same in both cases for both part-time and full-time students.

## PLACEMENT

Career resource staff are available from the Faculty of Business to assist students by helping them with their résumé and interviews and by directing them to career information on-campus. The Faculty of Business also handles all Co-op placements.

The University Student Placement Service handles all of the on-campus recruiting process except for the MBA Co-op placements. Up until the spring of 1991 the Canada Employment Centre ran the Placement Service. It has now been taken over by McMaster University.

The most active areas of business recruitment on-campus at McMaster are in the chemical industry, the financial sector, the pharmaceutical industry, and telecommunications.

## ON HAMILTON

The University is located on an attractive campus beside the Royal Botanical Gardens in West Hamilton. The campus is centred away from downtown in the area of Westdale. Buses run regularly, and you can be downtown in ten to fifteen minutes. Be advised that, if you are going to use your car, parking is poor. Robert Cooper, MBA '91, comments that "They are putting up buildings where parking lots used to be without replacing them. Also the enrolment at the university has increased. I think it's something they will have to deal with." Shuttles pass by every five to fifteen minutes, depending on the time of day, to pick people up from the parking lots furthest away. Parking is allocated on a seniority basis for student, staff, and faculty alike.

Most students live off-campus but close by. Co-op students sometimes swap accommodation while on work-terms since, while one half is taking classes, the other is on their work-term.

Hamilton is located on the southern shore of an inland harbour. The university and city rowing teams make good use of this. Ski hills are nearby, and Cootes Paradise is a marsh very close to campus where you can skate. Toronto is only forty minutes away.


## STUDENT PROFILES


### ISOBELLE GRAY
MBA '91

- Full-time student in the MBA program
- Four-year Honours BSc in Biology from the University of Windsor in 1980; MSc from the University of Windsor in 1987
- Worked for Environment Canada as a limnologist and for a private environmental consulting firm based in Guelph
- Looking for a commercial or industrial marketing position in the Toronto-Hamilton area
- Home town Montreal
- Married, no children

"I was looking for a school where they had a specific strength in marketing." Isobelle chose McMaster's MBA marketing stream. In her opinion, the marketing focus at McMaster is "more business to business than consumer marketing," and this is what she wanted.

Ken Deal, who taught Market Research, was one professor whose course Isobelle found especially worthwhile. "I have gained the most from projects. Cases are after the fact." In Deal's course, groups signed contracts with companies to provide them with market research. "It was handled very professionally . . . and it allowed you to find out if you wanted to work for the company or not."

Throughout Isobelle's MBA, she has had a number of teaching-assistant positions. At $2600 for ninety-six hours per term, this has helped her adjust to not having a full-time salary.

Has the MBA helped Isobelle? "Definitely, I wanted a career change. Before I went into the program I talked to a number of people, and it was fairly unanimous that if I wanted to get anywhere I had to get an MBA . . . I have learned a tremendous amount in a short period of time, and I have enjoyed the people I have met."

## RICHARD KUNG
MBA '92

- Co-op student in the MBA program
- Four-year BSc in Biochemistry from McMaster University in 1989
- Targeting the finance area of banking probably in the Toronto area
- Home town Hamilton
- Single

"After doing four years in Biochemistry, I did not want to continue in the sciences, but I did not have enough business experience to go right into the work force . . . I thought Co-op would give me about one year of work experience," comments Richard.

Richard is in the finance stream of the MBA program. "I wanted to work once in a bank and once for the government and private sectors to get a feeling for the different kinds of jobs available." However, Richard abandoned his original game plan of varied work placements after working for the CIBC. He really enjoyed the CIBC and wants to return there for subsequent placements.

Richard has been pleased with his placements. He comments on placements in general: "There are some good and bad jobs. If you don't like the job you don't go back next term and you learn from your experience."

"If I had gone into the full-time program I would have graduated right in the recession. Through the Co-op I have made some good contacts which will hopefully open doors."

# Memorial University of Newfoundland

---

■ **INQUIRIES**

MBA Program
Faculty of Business Administration
Memorial University of Newfoundland
St. John's, Newfoundland
A1B 3X5
(709) 737-8853

## FULL-TIME PROGRAM

■ **APPLICATION DEADLINE DATE FOR ADMISSIONS**

15 June for Canadian full-time applicants
15 May for Visa full-time applicants

■ **REQUIRED TO SUBMIT**

- GMAT score
- Official post-secondary transcripts
- TOEFL score is required from candidates whose first language is not English
- Three reference letters
- Personal statement

■ **AVERAGE GPA**

3.0 or B or 72%

■ **AVERAGE GMAT**

595 (Absolute minimum is 500)
If the GMAT is written more than once, the scores are not averaged

■ **PREFERENCE GIVEN TO A FOUR-YEAR DEGREE OVER A THREE-YEAR DEGREE?**

Only candidates with a four-year degree will be considered

- **NUMBER OF APPLICANTS**
  83

- **SIZE OF INCOMING CLASS**
  15

- **AVERAGE AGE OF STUDENTS**
  27.2

- **PERCENTAGE OF CLASS THAT ARE WOMEN**
  37%

- **DISTRIBUTION OF UNDERGRADUATE DEGREES**

  | | |
  |---|---|
  | BSc 38% | Other Undergraduate 13% |
  | BBA/BComm 19% | BA Humanities and |
  | BSc Engineering 19% | Social Sciences 11% |

Memorial University of Newfoundland is making its mark by becoming the school to beat in the Annual Concordia MBA Case Competition hosted by Concordia University. Eighteen MBA teams from graduate business schools were invited to participate in the 1991 National Competition. Memorial met the challenge and won first place in 1991, defending its 1988 and 1990 first place position. In 1989 they slipped only slightly and came in second. In 1988 and 1990 Memorial University of Newfoundland also won the Royal Bank Paper Writing Competition.

The case competition is taken seriously at Memorial. Their curriculum, however, offers a balanced approach of both theory and case, varying the approach according to the objectives of the course. In the majority of first-year courses, where the purpose is to impart fundamental theories and concepts, a conventional lecture/discussion approach is used. In second-year courses, and a few first-year courses, business cases are used to develop problem-solving and decision-making skills as well as to help integrate theory with practical application.

The focus of the program at the Memorial University of Newfoundland is that of general management. Concentrations in any area are not possible. However, students may elect to undertake research projects up to a value of three course credits to pursue research in specific areas of interest under the supervision of a faculty member.

The MBA program at Memorial University of Newfoundland can be taken on a full-time or part-time basis. The size of the MBA program is relatively small, allowing for class sizes of approximately eighteen to thirty-eight in required courses and eight to twenty-one students in electives. The MBA program at Memorial University of Newfoundland serves the needs of the province of Newfoundland with only approximately ten per cent of students coming from other areas in Canada and abroad. However, a wider geographic diversity is welcomed by the administration.

In 1987, second-year students were given the option of taking their first semester abroad at the Memorial University of Newfoundland's campus at Harlow in England. Professors and approximately ten to twelve students can be sent to Memorial University's campus in England. Although numbers have not warranted this opportunity in the last couple of years, it is still a possibility.

The Memorial University of Newfoundland is also the host to a number of institutes such as the P.J. Gardiner Institute for Small Business Studies, which has helped develop credit courses in small business management in the MBA and Bachelor of Commerce programs as well as self-help materials, workshops, and seminars on small-business operating problems and practices. In addition, the Institute occasionally hires an MBA student over the summer to operate a low-cost student consulting program for local small businesses. The Centre for Management Development is housed on the top floor of Memorial's business building and is the provincial focus for management education in Newfoundland for organizations of all types and managers at all levels.

When applying for admission, candidates may apply for advanced standing in the MBA program. Normally students would need two undergraduate courses in the subject to equal one at the graduate level with a minimum standing of 3.0 or B or 72%. The course in question should have been taken fairly recently. Typically three or four courses out of the possible twelve first-year courses are granted although up to ten have been given.

Also, in exceptional cases, candidates without undergraduate degrees but who meet all other requirements may be considered for admission. Preference is given to candidates who have a minimum of ten years of full-time managerial and executive experience, a high MEAN score, and university courses or professional credentials. Completion of certain undergraduate courses are often required prior to being considered for admission.

## PART-TIME PROGRAM

■ NOTE

Part-time students must be Canadian citizens or permanent residents

■ **APPLICATION DEADLINE DATE FOR ADMISSIONS**
15 June for September entry
1 November for January entry
1 April for May entry

■ **NUMBER OF APPLICANTS**
61

■ **SIZE OF INCOMING CLASS**
40

■ **AVERAGE AGE OF STUDENTS**
30.1

Students enrolled in the part-time MBA program at the Memorial University of Newfoundland have a maximum of seven years to complete their program. There is no mandatory minimum course load. Only one section of any course is offered, and the administration tries to rotate courses between day and night from year to year but, inevitably, part-time students cannot schedule all their classes at night.

When Memorial University of Newfoundland began to increase the number of full-time students in its MBA program a change in focus evolved. Cheryl Gallant, MBA '92, comments, "Originally the program catered to part-time students, but it doesn't so much now. A lot of core courses are offered during the day, and this is awkward."

Ken Dominie, MBA '91, wishes the administration would "make it more convenient for part-time students." Ken had to take every Monday afternoon off to take a required course since that was the only time it was offered. "Sometimes the choice of electives is not great," Ken adds. "At the stage I'm at now I have already taken a lot of them so this year I have taken one course outside of the faculty." Students are given the flexibility to take a maximum of two courses outside the Faculty of Business Administration.


## PLACEMENT

Placement is facilitated through the Canada Employment Centre. Eduardo Arambarri, MBA '91, comments, "Most students will probably end up leaving the island and go to the mainland because there isn't the employment on the island. Newfoundland's biggest export is people."

## ON ST. JOHN'S

St. John's has a metropolitan area population of 150,000 and is the capital city of the province of Newfoundland. The city is over four hundred years old — North America's oldest city — located on the boot-shaped harbour, which is the port of call for ships from around the world.

The campus is modern and about two hundred acres. It is situated about a thirty-minute brisk walk from downtown St. John's. Parking is atrocious. All the parking lots are a fair distance from the business building so you might be advised to take the bus. The building which houses the Faculty of Business Administration was recently expanded to twice its former size providing modern classrooms and lecture theatres, offices and discussion rooms, students' lounge, and microcomputer facilities.

Victorian architecture prevails in the city of St. John's, and in 1970 the older downtown area was restored. One student commented that it wasn't like being in a big city where if people don't know your name they won't give you the time of day.

If you are used to having access to Toronto, Montreal, or other large centres, you might feel a bit isolated on the island. It is an expensive effort to leave the island since you first have to pay the two hundred dollar flight to Halifax. However, if you like the outdoors, you can be in forested crown land just minutes out of the city.

## STUDENT PROFILES

*EDUARDO ARAMBARRI*
MBA '91

- Full-time student in the MBA program
- Five-year BSc Engineering (co-op) Mechanical from Memorial University of Newfoundland in 1987
- Worked for the National Research Council of Canada in Ottawa in their hydraulics lab
- Wants to remain in the engineering field perhaps with the Hibernia Project in Newfoundland
- Home town St. John's
- To be married in October

"I was really planning to do an MBA later when I was around thirty-five, but I talked to other people, and they told me how hard it was to juggle kids and a job."

Eduardo decided to do it now when he was single and did not have any debts. However, "I'm a little worried that I might be thrust right away into a management position," comments Eduardo.

The small size of the program was both an advantage and a disadvantage in Eduardo's opinion. There is a good rapport between profs and students. Also, "St. John's is a small city so you get a lot of contacts with the business community to help you with your projects."

On the negative side, however, the smallness of the program does not give students the opportunity to concentrate in any area. Also "The calendar shows a lot of courses but in reality quite a few are not offered since they have to have eight or ten students to be able to schedule that course."

Has the MBA helped Eduardo? "This remains to be seen. It has certainly helped me to think better and improve my writing and management skills, but I don't know yet if it will help my career." Eduardo adds, "There has been a lot of articles and talk lately about whether an MBA is worth it. Some companies will not hire an MBA and others think they are terrific."


## MIEN GALLANT
MBA '92

- Full-time then part-time student in the MBA program
- Four-year BSc in Chemistry from St. Francis Xavier University in 1988
- Works for the Department of Fisheries and Oceans in the Inspections Services Branch as an Operations Manager
- Employer pays for tuition, books, and gives some flexibility to take some classes during the day
- Hopes to get on the Department of Fisheries and Oceans fast-track leading to Deputy Minister level
- Home town Stephenville, Newfoundland
- Single

Mien is one of the four-member winning team in the Concordia MBA Case Competition. To be on the team you have to express an interest and be interviewed. Mien explains, "They are not just looking for the best presenters. The most important factor is being able to work together."

This is how she describes her experience in the competition. "It was mentally exhausting. Fourteen hours a day of hard mental work. It was the most gruelling but enjoyable part of my life."

Mien explains that each team is given case material to study and decide on a strategic plan. They were given three hours to prepare a forty-minute presentation, which they gave to a panel of "the board of directors." The board is made up of executives from the Montreal business community, who Mien says, "can pick the presentation apart or completely disagree with you. The Concordia Cup experience has helped me and my employer."

After applying to several MBA programs, Mien chose the one offered by Memorial University of Newfoundland. In her opinion, it has a generally strong faculty in most areas but especially in marketing and finance.

"The program originally catered to part-time students but it doesn't so much any more," mentions Mien. Comparing enrolments in 1988, Mien says, "Course sizes have dramatically gone up especially in required courses."

Taking courses with part-time students has been very beneficial for Mien. "We have great discussions in class. Just hearing the anecdotes of the part-time students is a learning experience. You are not just sitting there being lectured to. You are actively taking part."

"I would not have the position I have now without the MBA," states Mien.

# Université de Moncton

---

■ **INQUIRIES**

Doyen
Faculté d'administration
Université de Moncton
Moncton, New Brunswick
EIA 3E9
(506) 858-4205

## FULL-TIME PROGRAM

■ **APPLICATION DEADLINE DATE FOR ADMISSIONS**

Autumn session
- 15 June for Canadian students
- 1 February for foreign students

Winter session
- 15 November for Canadian students
- 1 September for foreign students

■ **REQUIRED TO SUBMIT**

- Official post-secondary transcripts
- TOEFL score is required from candidates whose first language is not English
- Reference letters
- Interest questionnaire

■ **AVERAGE GPA**

2.5/4.0 or B- or 65–70%

■ **AVERAGE GMAT**

Not required since the majority of students are French-speaking and the GMAT test is in English

- **PREFERENCE GIVEN TO A FOUR-YEAR DEGREE OVER A THREE-YEAR DEGREE?**

  Yes

- **NUMBER OF APPLICANTS**

  45

- **SIZE OF INCOMING CLASS**

  30

- **AVERAGE AGE OF STUDENTS**

  24

- **PERCENTAGE OF CLASS THAT ARE WOMEN**

  50%

- **PERCENTAGE OF CLASS WITH FULL-TIME WORK EXPERIENCE**

  25% (Average length of work experience is two years)

- **DISTRIBUTION OF UNDERGRADUATE DEGREES**

  BA Social Sciences 30%    BSc 10%
  BBA 30%                   BA 10%
  BSc Engineering 20%

- **OTHER RELATED PROGRAMS**

  MBA/LLB Program (started last year and Université de Moncton is the second university to offer it in the Maritimes) and Master of Public Administration

Outside of the province of Quebec, Université de Moncton offers the only French MBA program. It is not a bilingual program. Only three of the forty students enrolled this year are anglophones. Lectures are given primarily in French although most textbooks and written materials are in English.

The MBA program at the Université de Moncton primarily meets the needs of the province. Eighty per cent of its enrolment is drawn from the province of New Brunswick.

General management is the emphasis of the program, and there is no opportunity to concentrate in any one area. Three years ago the federal government created The Entrepreneurship Institute of the Atlantic Provinces in the Maritimes and located the regional office on-campus. The Institute's mandate is to help small businesses in the Maritimes and help students gain exposure to them. MBA students are hired by the institute in the summer to write cases involving small businesses, and students are encouraged to attend seminars offered by the institute.

The International Commerce Centre, founded by the federal government, is also located on the campus at the Université de Moncton. Similar to The Entrepreneurship Institute, there is no formal link to the MBA program, but students are encouraged to attend seminars offered through the centre.

Entrance scholarships are an attractive feature of the program. Approximately fifteen per cent of the class of 1990 received scholarships ranging in value from $2,000 to $5,000.

Reference letters are requested as part of the admission process. If the applicant has work experience, a letter from their supervisor would be preferred showing evidence that the applicant can work in groups. If the applicant has no work experience, then a reference from a professor should attest to how the student can think logically and solve problems. A statistics course is a mandatory requirement of the program.

The administration at the Université de Moncton purposely tries to attract students from not only business but engineering and the social sciences as well.

## PART-TIME PROGRAM

■ **NUMBER OF APPLICANTS**
45

■ **SIZE OF INCOMING CLASS**
30

■ **AVERAGE AGE OF STUDENTS**
30

The MBA program has three semesters, and students can apply almost anytime. To ensure admission before the term starts it is advisable to apply at least one month prior to the time you would like to start classes. The maximum time limit for students to complete the MBA program at the Université de Moncton is seven years.

The administration advises part-time students, who are also working full-time, to take a maximum of two courses per semester. Students have the option of taking courses either during the evening or the day and are in the same classes as the full-time students.

Students who could only take courses in the evening comment that "Some people have not been able to take classes for one semester because of the lack of courses available."

## PLACEMENT

A Canada Employment Centre is located on-campus and facilitates placement for all of the programs at the Université de Moncton including the MBA program. Some of the organizations that recruit on campus are the Federal and Provincial Government, Irving, New Brunswick Power, New Brunswick Tel, and Xerox.

The MBA students themselves informally launched a campaign to increase the visibility of the program by sending out 250 letters to corporations in New Brunswick, Quebec, Toronto, and Vancouver with information about the school and the program along with résumés of the graduating class. Geraldine Harrigan comments, "The majority of companies do not come on-campus. Most students apply on their own."

## ON MONCTON

Moncton has a population of 70,000, and the campus of the Université de Moncton is in the heart of the city. It is a twenty-minute walk downtown from the campus or, if you want to take the bus, the transit system is good. It is easy to find accommodation, and a typical one-bedroom apartment is around $350 per month. Residence accommodation is also available on-campus. A nice feature about the library is that the MBA students have their own study carrels.

It is a small town, where the pace is slower than in a big city like Montreal, and the people are friendly.

## STUDENT PROFILES

*GERALDINE HARRIGAN*
MBA '91

- Full-time and then part-time student in the MBA program
- Four-year BNSc from the Université de Moncton in 1980

- Nursed in a hospital experienced in the areas of intensive care, infection control, and employee health nurse
- Keeping doors open and watching for opportunities in general management
- Home town Campbellton

Geraldine was one of the few anglophone students enrolled in the MBA program at the Université de Moncton. The opportunity to attend a French-speaking school improved Geraldine's French-speaking skills. The combination of speaking French and reading English helps anglophones and francophones alike. Most people "arrive unilingual French, but by the time they finished they are bilingual because a lot of the written material is in English," comments Geraldine.

Regarding teaching, Geraldine would like some of the professors to demonstrate more current applications. One professor that Geraldine, and others interviewed, thought was very good at associating theory and practice was Claude Des Rocher who taught Operational Research.

The generalist focus of the program was exactly what Geraldine wanted. ". . . for people without a background in administration, it gives you an overview of all the management areas," states Geraldine.

Geraldine believes that the MBA is going to help her to work in the area of administration. However, she advises that "All university gives you the working tools, and then it's up to the student to function one hundred per cent in the work place. It is up to you to prove that you are able to live up to expectations."


*SYLVAIN LEVESQUE*
MBA '91

- Full-time student in the MBA program
- Four-year BBA from the Université de Moncton in 1989
- Looking for a general management position in the banking community in Quebec
- Home town Chateaugay, Quebec, near Montreal
- Single

Sylvain has no full-time work experience. He went right from his undergraduate degree in Business Administration into his MBA, and if he had to do it over again he would.

During the summer, Sylvain managed a painting franchise where he had thirteen employees working for him and made $55,000 in sales. He was able to relate a lot of what happened that summer to what he was learning in the MBA program.

He chose to stay at the Université de Moncton to do his MBA because he was given advance standing in some courses, which enabled him to finish his MBA in one and a half years.

For Sylvain, the biggest strength of the program was the group work and the presentations. "They increased my confidence level and improved my speaking skills." Also, the small class sizes enhanced the relationships between students and profs.

Where could the program improve? "There is little funding available to send students to compete in case competitions or conferences and meetings," states Sylvain.

Although Sylvain had an undergraduate degree in Administration, he still believes that the MBA was useful. "I've learned how to manage my time, and it has helped me to look at problems in more depth."

# University of New Brunswick

■ **INQUIRIES**

    MBA Program
    Faculty of Administration
    University of New Brunswick
    Fredericton, New Brunswick
    E3B 5A3
    (506) 453-4869

## FULL-TIME PROGRAM

■ **APPLICATION DEADLINE DATE FOR ADMISSIONS**

    31 May
    However, good applications are considered after this deadline

■ **REQUIRED TO SUBMIT**

- GMAT score
- Official post-secondary transcripts
- TOEFL score is required from candidates whose first language is not English
- Three reference letters
- Résumé

■ **AVERAGE GPA**

    3.4 (Minimum is 3.0/4.3) or B or 72%

■ **AVERAGE GMAT**

    530 (Minimum score is 450 if offset by a higher GPA)
    If the GMAT is written more than once, the most recent GMAT score is used

■ **PREFERENCE GIVEN TO A FOUR-YEAR DEGREE OVER A THREE-YEAR DEGREE?**

    Yes

Additional degrees, diplomas, or graduate courses are looked on favourably

- **NUMBER OF APPLICANTS**
  80

- **SIZE OF INCOMING CLASS**
  30

- **AVERAGE AGE OF STUDENTS**
  Approximately 28

- **PERCENTAGE OF CLASS THAT ARE WOMEN**
  Approximately 30%

- **PERCENTAGE OF CLASS WITH FULL-TIME WORK EXPERIENCE**
  90% (Average length of work experience is two years)

- **DISTRIBUTION OF UNDERGRADUATE DEGREES**
  BA Social Sciences and BBA 50%
  BSc Engineering 35%
  BEd, BFA, and Other Undergraduate 15%

- **OTHER RELATED PROGRAMS**
  Diploma of Administrative Studies and Master of Public Administration

The University of New Brunswick's MBA program is a small and relatively young program founded in 1986. The majority of its students come from the province of New Brunswick, and they enjoy good student/faculty interaction in small class sizes of twenty to thirty and five to ten in elective courses. The teaching style takes on a balanced approach of mostly lecture in first year, then shifting to a case approach in the second year. On the qualitative versus quantitative scale, the program falls to the quantitative side of the middle. A score in the upper forty percentile on the quantitative section of the GMAT is preferred. This is especially noted if an applicant does not have any calculus background.

A broad knowledge base is the foundation of the University of New Brunswick's MBA program. If students wish to gain expertise in a certain area, they have that opportunity by choosing to do a thesis or a project report. At present there are no formal areas of concentration except for Transportation

Management. Informal specializations can be arranged by choosing elective courses in the areas of Finance, Human Resource Management, Industrial Relations, International Business, Marketing, and Quantitative Methods.

Students enrolled in the MBA program at the University of New Brunswick share a common course of study with the Master of Public Administration students in the first year of the program. In the second year, MBA students pursue a more specialized education in the private sector while Master of Public Administration students choose courses related to the public sector.

The MBA and Master of Public Administration programs are located on the Fredericton campus where they are offered on both a full-time and part-time basis. The first year of the program is also offered on the Saint John Campus.

Some changes in the program are in the process of review, and if approved they will be in effect by September 1992. It has been proposed that the Master of Public Administration program be discontinued and replaced by a concentration in Public Administration of four to five courses within the MBA degree. This is a result of more students opting for the MBA. Also, M. Rashid, Assistant Dean — Graduate Studies, comments that "In two years' time Entrepreneurship, International Business, Human Resources, and Finance are being looked at as possible areas of concentration."

A significant percentage of the faculty have international backgrounds. The globalization of business is further strengthened by the Faculty's Centre of International Marketing and Entrepreneurship and the several courses available in international business.

Applied skills are stressed in ten compulsory communication skills workshops offered in the first term of each year and a computer literacy workshop taken in September. Practical skills are honed in the summer internship program. Firms and provincial and federal departments in the cities of Fredericton and St. John are contacted and informed of the program. Four to five students every year are given the opportunity to work on projects within the public and private sectors over the summer months. The students are monitored, assessed both on their job performance and written report. The students receive a course credit for the internship.

Since 1986 the MBA program has emphasized small business in its curriculum. In 1988 the Centre of International Marketing and Entrepreneurship was founded by the New Brunswick and Federal governments. The Centre encourages student and faculty research in small business and entrepreneurship. In addition, the University of New Brunswick offers two optional core courses in Small Business and Entrepreneurship.

In Rashid's opinion, if you are looking for "a balanced and dynamic curriculum, emphasis on computer literacy and communications skills, globalization, small class sizes, a reputed faculty, an Internship program, excellent library and computer facilities, and a congenial and stimulating environment, then the Faculty of Administration at the University of New Brunswick is the place for you."

## PART-TIME PROGRAM

■ NUMBER OF APPLICANTS
60

■ SIZE OF INCOMING CLASS
45

■ AVERAGE AGE OF STUDENTS
Approximately 35

Normally six years is the maximum time limit for part-time students to complete their MBA at the University of New Brunswick. Part-time students can choose to take classes in the day or during the evening. Courses offered are rotated between day and night for part-time students. Part-time and full-time students are integrated in the classes.

The Saint John campus is almost exclusively geared to part-time students since only the first year of the MBA is offered in Saint John. Michael Frauley, a part-time MBA '93 student, comments that "Accessibility of courses is definitely a problem resulting in a one-and-a-half hour drive to the Fredericton campus. Having to travel seventy miles is something of a curse."

Michael Frauley also describes the atmosphere on the Saint John campus as different compared to Fredericton's campus. "The Saint John campus has more students around thirty years old, and the classes are more interactive, whereas in Fredericton there are more full-time students right out of undergrad. The full-time students tend to be more timid, and there is less interaction in class."

## PLACEMENT

The Canada Employment Centre facilitates placement for all students attending the University of New Brunswick. However, they are in the process of developing a full-fledged in-house placement service for MBA and BBA students.

At present federal and provincial government departments, banks, and other financial institutions such as London Life, recruit on-campus.

## ON FREDERICTON AND SAINT JOHN

Fredericton has a population of 40,000. It is a very pretty non-industrial town with an economic base supported mostly by the university and government offices. The campus is located downtown. From the gates of the university to the St. John River and the main street of Fredericton, it is only five blocks.

The tempo of the city is laid back. There are no traffic jams, and you can be out in the country within five minutes of downtown.

Saint John is seventy miles from Fredericton. Unlike Fredericton, it is an industrial city with a couple of breweries, shipping, oil refining, and pulp and paper. It is a relatively small city, and the students describe the people as friendly.

## STUDENT PROFILES

*CHRISTIAN LEVESQUE*
MBA '91

- Full-time student in the MBA program
- Four-year BA in Political Science from the University of New Brunswick in 1989
- Targeting marketing positions in the public sector in central or eastern Canada
- Home town Fredericton
- Single

Christian made the decision to go directly into the MBA program from his undergraduate degree without full-time work experience. "I would definitely go right through again since I would have had a hard time quitting a job and living without a salary."

The small class size and personalized approach of the faculty were a strength of the program in Christian's opinion.

The program is young, however, and Christian has found "a lack of a common vision within the faculty itself. Everyone has their own ideas of what the program should be. It is hard to get a consensus, so it leads to a conservative approach. They should be more pro-active."

The MBA has definitely helped Christian. "I am learning things now that would have taken me a lot longer to learn in the business world. Now I know what field of business I want to go into and which ones I don't like."


BARB WISHART
MBA '91

- Full-time then part-time student in the MBA program
- Four-year Bachelor of Teaching from the University of New Brunswick; one-year BEd from the University of New Brunswick in 1975; two-year MEd from the University of New Brunswick in 1980
- Taught French in junior high schools for twenty years
- Has accepted the position of Executive Director of the New Brunswick Dental Society
- Home is on the Grand Manan Island in the Bay of Fundy
- Married, with two children

Barb says she took the MBA because "The MBA was an out from teaching, and the MBA was the most marketable tool." However, even when Barb was full-time in the MBA program, she continued to teach half time. She never stopped working during the program. Barb has an incredibly high energy level, and she was very determined to finish her MBA.

As a part-time student, Barb looked at the degree as "a trial in survival. It was not so much mentally challenging as it was challenging to your stamina."

In Barb's opinion, "The bulk of the University of New Brunswick's students are part-time but the program is geared to full-time students. Most of the courses are offered during the day (on the Fredericton campus), and therefore I have had to drive to the Saint John Campus."

To Barb, the strength of the program lies in its small size. "The professors take the time; they know who we are."

Barb explains what the MBA had done for her. "I did not have any idea of what I was walking into. I just dug in and taught myself. The MBA has taught me how to deal with the unknown." Barb continues on to say, "I got my present job because of my MBA."

# University of Ottawa/
# Université d'Ottawa

---

■ **INQUIRIES**

Graduate Programmes
Faculty of Administration
University of Ottawa/Université d'Ottawa
136 Jean-Jacques Lussier
Ottawa, Ontario
KIN 6N5
(613) 564-7004

## FULL-TIME PROGRAM

■ **APPLICATION DEADLINE DATE FOR ADMISSIONS**

1 March

■ **REQUIRED TO SUBMIT**

- GMAT score is optional and recommended for candidates with a marginal academic standing
- Official post-secondary transcripts
- TOEX score is required from candidates whose first language is not English
- Two reference letters
- Résumé

■ **AVERAGE GPA**

3.2 or B+ or 75%

■ **AVERAGE GMAT**

550–580

The GMAT is optional and recommended for candidates with a marginal academic standing to improve their chances of admission. If the GMAT is written more than once, the best score is used

■ **PREFERENCE GIVEN TO A FOUR-YEAR DEGREE OVER A THREE-YEAR DEGREE?**

No
However, more emphasis will be placed on academic requirements or work experience for applicants with a three-year degree

■ **NUMBER OF APPLICANTS**

494

■ **SIZE OF INCOMING CLASS**

90

■ **AVERAGE AGE OF STUDENTS**

25

■ **PERCENTAGE OF CLASS THAT ARE WOMEN**

50%

■ **OTHER RELATED PROGRAMS**

Diploma of Administrative Studies, MBA (International), MBA/LLB, MBA/LLL, Master of Engineering Management, MHA (Master of Health Administration), and Master of System Science

In a 10 October 1989 interview with the Ottawa *Citizen*, David Zussman, Dean of the Faculty of Administration, emphasizes that "The school is called 'administration' because its public sector component is just as important." The Summer of 1990 "Report on the MBA Alumni Survey" supports his claim. Fifty-three per cent of its alumni in the Ottawa-Hull area are employed in the public sector, thirty-two per cent in the private sector. David Zussman himself has extensive experience with the government and is a nationally recognized authority on public service management and public policy. Prior to accepting the position of Dean of the Faculty of Administration in 1988, he was Senior Departmental Policy Advisor to Jean Chrétien, who was, then, Secretary of State for External Affairs.

"The school has one foot in the business world and one foot in administration — juggling the two *en deux langues*," Dean Zussman comments in another article in the Ottawa *Citizen* (10 October 1989). The atmosphere at the University of Ottawa/Université d'Ottawa and in the city of Ottawa itself is definitely bilingual. However, more than two-thirds of the MBA student population is anglophone. The traffic and building signs are in French first, then English. The support staff and administration converse easily in French but are quick to switch to English when speaking to an anglophone. However, French and English are not language requirements, and you do not have to be bilingual to take an MBA at the University of Ottawa/ Université d'Ottawa. French is required only at the undergraduate level. All the core courses and approximately ninety per cent of the electives are offered in English. There is more likely to be a problem if you are a francophone who cannot speak English.

"We're one of Ottawa's best kept secrets. We haven't done much of a job informing the public of what we are about. . . . We're quite proud of our grads — we just have to figure out how to tell our story," David Zussman comments in the Ottawa *Citizen* (10 October 1989). The University of Ottawa/Université d'Ottawa's MBA program founded in 1968 is still relatively young. Now, however, they are becoming more pro-active — a new International Management Stream will be introduced in 1991, an Executive program is planned for 1992, and a proposal for a PhD program in Management is in the planning stage.

The University of Ottawa/Université d'Ottawa offers strong expertise in the international area. Fifty to sixty per cent of the professors are from other countries, twenty languages are represented, and some faculty do consulting in other countries. According to Pat Johnston, Assistant to the Dean, "This international focus has been around for a long time, and over time it has become more focused. It has been an evolution rather than a recent decision."

As a result a new International Management Stream within the existing MBA program has been developed and the first class will begin the program in September 1991. The first class will have an enrolment of approximately thirty to forty students with a maximum enrolment of fifty in the future. Fifty per cent of the class will come from abroad, and this will be an integral part of the program. This is a truly international environment in terms of faculty, students, languages spoken, and work internships abroad.

The development of the International Stream was encouraged and supported by the Faculty of Administration's Business Advisory Board and the business community. The Director of the International Stream is Jean-Emile Denis, who was a visiting professor at the International Institute for Management Development in Europe and on the faculty of Ecole des Hautes Etudes Commerciales, University of Montreal, for a number of years. In Denis's opinion, "European programs are way beyond North American Schools," so they used them as a model but added North American content.

The new International Stream will be only twelve months long, similar to

European programs. The core business courses covered in the first year of the regular MBA are still required, but students have to have completed them prior to admission. Therefore, first year MBA students of any university program or students who have completed their Bachelor of Commerce can apply. For the International stream only, candidates must be bilingual in French and English and a third language is an asset. Approximately fifty per cent of the courses will be taught in French, although exams can be written in either language.

The courses taught in the International Stream are completely separate from the mainstream MBA partly due to the modular design of the courses. A student in the regular MBA cannot take the International Stream courses and vice versa. Instead of all courses having the same weight and length, they will vary from one to three credits depending on their importance. Organizing the courses into modules of varying length facilitates the presentation of material in a logical sequence and aids integration across topics. The teaching methods are more simulations and pedagogical techniques. The "soft skills" of teamwork, leadership, and communication will be stressed.

The University of Ottawa/Université d'Ottawa is working with CIDA, Export Development, and External Affairs for feedback and internships. Part of the twelve-month program is a ten-to-twelve week work internship abroad during the summer. The foreign student contingent will be placed in internships with an international scope within Canada.

The University of Ottawa/Université d'Ottawa offers the traditional areas of concentration from private, public, and social sectors, gaining expertise in accounting, finance, human resources management, information systems, international management, marketing, and operations research.

A mandatory requirement of the MBA program at the University of Ottawa/Université d'Ottawa is a math course in linear algebra and calculus. For students who are lacking this background, the Faculty offers a review course which can be taken at night.

Candidates with university courses that have equivalent content to that covered in an MBA course, or have a Bachelor of Commerce, may apply for advanced standing. A student with a Bachelor of Commerce can apply for an advanced standing in a maximum of nine courses. As a general rule, a candidate must have an honours degree or its equivalent to be eligible to receive advanced standing, and a grade equal to a "B" or 70% in the course. Students with a three-year degree can apply for exemptions where they can substitute an upper-year course or an elective for the credit they have taken at another institution.

## PART-TIME PROGRAM

■ **NUMBER OF APPLICATIONS**
295

■ **SIZE OF INCOMING CLASS**
132

■ **AVERAGE AGE OF THE STUDENTS**
32

The University of Ottawa/Université d'Ottawa requires part-time students to complete the MBA program within a maximum of six years, and they are required to take a minimum course load of one course. Classes are held in the evening starting as early as 4:00 p.m.

Yvonne Chow, MBA '92, feels that the course availability and selection was poor, especially in the summer term. "Sometimes courses are not offered, and I have had to wait twelve months to take it." Yvonne suggests that the administration "should ask students what they want to take before they schedule the courses."

## PLACEMENT

In 1987 the Faculty of Administration recognized that the Canada Employment Centre (CEC) was suffering from budget cutbacks. The manager of the CEC, who provided placement support for the entire student population, had no secretarial or computer support. Therefore, the faculty established an in-house Placement Service. The CEC may close in the spring of 1991, and the university is negotiating with officials from the Canada Employment Centre. However, at the time when this research was being done, nothing had been decided. This ambiguity may affect the class of 1993.

The in-house placement service provides and distributes one thousand résumé books of the graduating MBA class to the private and public sector in Toronto, Montreal, and Ottawa. In addition to employment with the public sector, a large number of students will find employment in the areas of consulting, finance, management, and marketing in the private sector.

# ON OTTAWA

The campus of the University of Ottawa/Université d'Ottawa is situated in the heart of downtown, a ten-minute walk from the Rideau Centre, the Market, and the Rideau Canal. For nightlife, Hull is just across the river, and the bars are open until 3 a.m. On weekends, students head off for the many ski resorts within a forty-five-minute drive.

Housing is available within close proximity to the campus, but this isn't really an issue because the transit system is so good. Simon Brault, MBA '91, describes it as "the Number 1 transportation system in North America. You can live far away from campus if you want, and it only takes fifteen minutes to get to school." The campus is on the route of the transit-way, a highway that only buses can use. During peak hours, the bus costs $1.90, and at other times it costs ninety-five cents.

Kara Moors, MBA '91, comments on how living in a bilingual city and going to a bilingual school has affected her. "I operate the same way. I speak English all the time although I have learned a few words in French. You have to make the effort to learn French. It does make you aware, however, of francophone and international perspectives."

## STUDENT PROFILES

### PHILIPPE MARLEAU
MBA '91

- Full-time student in the MBA program
- Three-year BSc in Biochem and a three-year Bachelor of Social Sciences from the University of Ottawa/Université d'Ottawa in 1989
- Short-term goal is to work as a nursing home inspector, or in government relations, or consulting
- Long-term goal is to own and operate homes for the elderly
- Home town Ottawa
- Single

Philippe did not apply anywhere else. "I love the city of Ottawa and the fact that it's bilingual."

However, it was a toss-up for Philippe between the Master of Health Administration and the MBA at the University of Ottawa/Université d'Ottawa. He chose the MBA because "Anything I could do with the MHA I could do with the MBA." Also, Ottawa's MBA program is flexible enough to allow Philippe to take electives in the MHA program.

When asked what were some of the strengths of the program, Philippe spoke highly of the international focus. He mentioned that over half of the faculty had studied abroad or had native origins overseas. This combined with a bilingual atmosphere was definitely an asset in Philippe's opinion.

According to Philippe, there were opportunities to work for the government. A number of the professors have worked in the federal government and bring their experiences to the classroom.

Attracting quality French students was something Philippe felt quite strongly about, and he felt the program could improve by offering more courses in French.

Philippe was one of the youngest in the program, and he did not have any prior full-time work experience. He observes that, "People with work experience could add to case discussions, and I learned from them. I don't feel it was a disadvantage and would still go directly from undergraduate and get it over with quickly."


*TOBY TAYLOR*
MBA '93

- Part-time student in the MBA program
- Four-year BA in Psychology and Math from St. Francis Xavier University in 1986
- Hired by a computer graphics firm to work in technical sales
- Changed jobs in 1989 to work with IBM as a Systems Engineering Representative
- Plans to continue working for IBM upon graduation
- Home town Newcastle, New Brunswick
- Married, no children

"I am doing the MBA for personal interest rather than career development. At IBM it isn't a factor in promotion." IBM "bases their decision on the person's qualities, and if you don't have the education they train you internally."

Toby started the MBA in 1988, and, upon successful completion of her courses, IBM reimburses her for her tuition and books.

In Toby's opinion, the program had some good professors and some that were not. She defines a good professor as "one that came from industry. It's easy to identify with them. Others were purely academic and wanted their course to be the most important thing in your life."

As a part-time student, Toby found it difficult to find courses that she had the prerequisites for. "This term I could only take one course although I would have really liked to have taken two." Scheduling of some courses at 4:00 p.m. was also a limiting factor for Toby who could not get to campus from work that early.

Toby has gained personal satisfaction and knowledge from the MBA but "Having the degree won't be anything magical when I'm finished. I don't know if an MBA does anything for you professionally except make you well rounded. Even if you have a job at the bottom of the ladder you should be aware of what is going on."

# Université du Québec à Montréal

■ **INQUIRIES**

Executive MBA Program/MBA Research Program
Université du Québec à Montréal
Boîte Postale 8888, Station A
Montréal, Québec
H3C 3P8
Executive: (514) 987-7704
Research: (514) 987-4448

## *FULL-TIME PROGRAM*

■ **APPLICATION DEADLINE DATE FOR ADMISSIONS**

Executive MBA Program:   30 November for courses
                                            beginning next May

MBA Research Program:   1 April for courses beginning
                                            next September

■ **REQUIRED TO SUBMIT**

- Official post-secondary transcripts
- Three reference letters
- Letter of intent
- For Executive program only:  Résumé
                                                     Personal interview

■ **AVERAGE GPA**

3.0 or B or 75%

■ **AVERAGE GMAT**

A GMAT score may be required in the Executive program to clarify
marginal cases but it is not routinely used in the decision-making
process for admission. The difference in language and culture make
it of limited relevance.

- **PREFERENCE GIVEN TO A FOUR-YEAR DEGREE OVER A THREE-YEAR DEGREE?**

  No

- **NUMBER OF APPLICANTS**

  400 Executive MBA    219 MBA Research

- **SIZE OF INCOMING CLASS**

  150 Executive MBA    102 MBA Research

- **AVERAGE AGE OF STUDENTS**

  37 Executive MBA    26 MBA Research

- **PERCENTAGE OF CLASS THAT ARE WOMEN**

  40% Executive MBA    57% MBA Research

- **PERCENTAGE OF CLASS WITH FULL-TIME WORK EXPERIENCE**

  For the Executive MBA 100% (A minimum of four years work experience is required. The average length of work experience is ten years.) For the MBA Research work experience is not required and less than 10% of the student body have work experience.

- **DISTRIBUTION OF UNDERGRADUATE DEGREES**

  Executive MBA:

  | | |
  |---|---|
  | BSc Engineering 9% | BEd 6% |
  | BSc Math and Science 22% | LLB 1% |
  | BBA 30% | ECO 4% |
  | BA Arts and Social Sciences 17% | |

  MBA Research:

  | | |
  |---|---|
  | BBA 75% | BSc Engineering 11% |
  | BSc Math & Science 13% | LLB 1% |

- **OTHER BACKGROUNDS**

  Executive MBA:

  | | |
  |---|---|
  | No bachelor's degree 5% | Certificate 12% |

  MBA Research:

  | | |
  |---|---|
  | No bachelor's degree 0% | Certificate 0% |

- **OTHER RELATED PROGRAMS**

  Master of Public Administration, MSc in Accounting, MSc Administration in Management and Information Science, MSc Project Management, and PhD

The official language of instruction at the Université du Québec à Montréal is French. Competency in English is also required since a large part of the textbooks and case studies are written in English. Candidates more fluent in English than in French can write their essays and exams in that language.

A choice of two MBA programs is available at the Université du Québec à Montréal: an MBA Research program and an Executive MBA. The MBA Research program at the Université du Québec à Montréal is more typical of a Master of Science program than an MBA. Denis Gervais, Co-ordinator for Graduate Studies at the Department of Administrative Science, says, "We develop specialists." Students can concentrate in one of ten specializations: Finance, Industrial Relations, Management, Management of Information Systems, Marketing, Organizational Behaviour, Personnel, Production, Real Estate and Land Management, and Strategy. The two-year program consists of core courses that are borrowed from the Executive MBA program, three courses in their specialty, two courses preparing students for a thesis, and a thesis.

The MBA Research program was developed initially to provide the Université du Québec à Montréal business students with an opportunity to continue their studies at a higher level. This orientation still exists, although a few candidates from other universities are accepted. The program was designed for students to enter directly after the completion of their undergraduate degree in business areas. Work experience is not required, and most of the emphasis for admission is placed on academic standing. After completing the program, the majority of graduates are employed as consultants. Some of them continue at the PhD level, competing for academic positions.

In contrast, the Executive MBA is a generalist program intended for middle to senior management as well as junior executives with at least four years of relevant work experience. Unlike most executive programs, a degree is granted, and it is one year in length (starting in April and ending the following April) consisting of forty-five credits. The short duration of the program does not allow for the development of concentrations. However, the possibility exists for some students, with the appropriate backgrounds, to take specialized courses in the MBA Research or Master of Project Management programs.

The admission process for the Executive MBA program includes interviewing almost all of the applicants. This is a very time-consuming process, but P. D'Aragon, Director of the Executive MBA Program, feels quite strongly that it is the most important factor affecting admission. During the interview, a candidate's ability to relate to people is assessed as well as how they operate under pressure. Prerequisites to the Executive MBA program are courses in basic accounting and mathematics, computer ability, and management experience.

The admission process for the MBA Research program does not include an interview. However, after the students have been admitted, they are invited for a group interview to facilitate a matching process with areas of specialization and, if possible, to a professor who could eventually be their thesis director.

## PART-TIME EXECUTIVE MBA PROGRAM
### (No part-time MBA Research program)

■ SIZE OF INCOMING CLASS

55

■ PERCENTAGE OF CLASS THAT ARE WOMEN

30%

Most students enrolled in the part-time Executive MBA program are required to enrol as full-time students for a minimum of four months as a residency requirement. In the spring of 1991 an experimental program was initiated at the Université du Québec's Laval campus, where thirty-eight students will complete their program on a part-time basis entirely. In the last four years the percentage of enrolment comprised of part-time students has dramatically increased by five times. To meet the needs of this new direction, the administration has increased the number of courses available during the evening.

The maximum time limit for part-time students to complete the Executive MBA program is three years with a minimum course load of two courses per session.

The MBA Research program is opened only to full-time students. However, it is possible for students to complete their thesis on a part-time basis.

## PLACEMENT

The Business programs of the Department of Administrative Science have their own placement function, which provides job-search support in terms of résumé and interview preparation. A weakness of the program is the on-campus recruiting function, which has little activity due to the lack of personnel dedicated to it. A Canada Employment Centre is not available to augment the department's services. However, because of the older age of the student body and the significant work experience, most of the student body have already developed an established network of contacts that can help them in their job search.

The MBA students invite local people in business to speak on current topics. This provides students with valuable information but also an opportunity to meet with "would be" employers on an informal basis. Students also organize a mailing out of students' résumés. Participation of the students in this service is voluntary. A part of this activity is sponsored by the business programs.

## ON MONTREAL

Université du Québec à Montréal is a large university with a student population of approximately 38,000. The architecture is mostly modern, and the campus is intermixed with Montreal's business sector. In fact, the building that houses the Faculty of Business is in a high-rise where many storeys are occupied by office space. Several students commented that the university was not in the best of neighbourhoods and that safety was a factor at night.

In the summer of 1991, the Department of Administrative Science will be moving to its own building. The existing space does provide MBA students with their own lounge which can serve as a conference room. Funding for the lounge was made possible primarily by RCMP Accounting Firm. Université du Québec à Montréal MBA students also have their own study rooms, access to a phone, and on occasion a fax machine.

## STUDENT PROFILES

### GREGORY HARDY
MBA '91

- Full-time student in the Executive MBA program
- Three-year BA in Psychology from McGill University in 1988
- Worked for four years full-time during his undergraduate degree
- Involved in production with the textile industry in Montreal
- Focusing on a managerial position within the automotive industry upon graduation
- Home town Montreal
- Single

For Gregory, there were many reasons why he chose the Université du Québec à Montréal to do his MBA. It was less expensive, his family was located in Montreal, and he felt that it was an advantage to have another working language besides English.

Gregory described the atmosphere at Université du Québec à Montréal's MBA program as "more camaraderie than cut throat competition. We use our varied backgrounds to help each other." He explains that the administration was also supportive. "There is a strong team effort. The school fits the structure of the program to the individual student."

When asked where the program could improve, Gregory was quite satisfied but he mentions that "The administration tries to keep class sizes down, but there could be a slight improvement if they had more faculty."

Gregory concludes, "Education in the business world is really a never ending process. When you finish your MBA you realize that you are not finished learning. It gives you a good base of education and opportunities to take advantage of new developments, new technology, and new innovations as a result of a strong base."

*IRENE NAULT*
MBA '92

- Part-time student in the Executive MBA program
- Has several university courses but does not have an undergraduate degree
- Worked in the banking field for three years, the insurance field for ten, and was a consultant in data processing for six
- Presently the Assistant Vice-President in Planning System Information, Architecture of Information Systems and Control Area with Montreal Trust
- Home town Fortierville, Quebec (between Quebec City and Trois Rivières)
- Single

While some MBA's are eager to climb the corporate ladder, Irène has already done that. Irène comments, "I have been under pressure for a long time with a lot of responsibility. The MBA will permit me to live in a rural area where I can work in administration, perhaps in a retirement home, or as a university instructor."

Irène appreciated the fact that Université du Québec à Montréal looked more at her experience than the fact that she did not have a degree. She had considered applying to Concordia but their executive program would have been ten to fifteen thousand dollars more. Irène applied to Université du Québec à Montréal, passed a qualifying exam and interview, and started the Executive program.

The Executive MBA program at Université du Québec à Montréal is a good one, in Irène's opinion. What really interested Irène were the applied courses. She mentions that "At the same time you are learning the theory, you can see if it really works in the work place."

One opportunity Irène had to test out the theory was in Professor Y. Allaire's Strategic Planning course which she thought was excellent. "I was currently involved in developing a strategic plan in my work, and I was able to apply it right away," says Irène. Professor P. D'Aragon's class in Operations in Manufacturing was another class that Irène, and other students interviewed, found to be well taught and applied in nature. However, Irène adds that "There weren't as many applied courses as I thought there would be."

From a part-time student's perspective, Irène believes that the administration was responsive to requests for courses to be offered in the summer sessions. However, she feels that the administration still used a full-time frame of reference in terms of their expectations of part-time students. "They ask part-time students to follow the same arrangement of group work even though we have other time commitments," Irène says.

"The MBA has helped me, not so much for management skills, because I already had them, but more in terms of planning models and the accounting side, where I got a greater depth of knowledge. I have been able to grow with it," Irène states.


*MARJORIE BIRABEN*
MBA '92

- Full-time student in the MBA Research program specializing in marketing in terms of tourism
- Three-year BComm/BBA with a concentration in Tourism from Université du Québec à Montréal in 1990
- Intends to pursue her PhD with a services-marketing orientation in Europe
- Home town Montreal
- Single

In Marjorie's second year she will have only one course and will then concentrate on her thesis "Positioning and Differentiation of Touristic Regions of Quebec."

Marjorie chose the MBA Research program, and "looking back at my choice I don't regret it. The Executive program is more geared to people who have work experience in different areas, and want to acquire business tools. I wanted something that would challenge me and teach me more about research. I felt the Executive program would have duplicated, to some extent, the material I learned in my business undergraduate degree," says Marjorie.

The program is taught in French, but the majority of written material is in English. "I was able to read English before entering the program, but reading a newspaper or magazine is different than reading at this level. There was a period of transition required," comments Marjorie.

Marjorie emphasizes the excellence of the faculty. She notes that they had a lot of experience in the private sector but their primary concern is research. Many, including J.C. Chebat and C. Dussard, have won awards for their publications and research.

An opportunity to have more courses in her specialization was something that Marjorie would have liked.

"I'm happy with what I did and the global focus of the program. The teachers are very accessible to the students and involve us in their research."


*SYLVIE PARADIS*
MBA '92

- Full-time student in the MBA Research program with a specialty in Marketing
- Three-year BA in Tourism from Université du Québec à Montréal in 1989
- Worked for the City of Montreal as a market analyst
- Took the first year of a Master of Science in Marketing at Ecoles des Hautes Etudes Commerciales
- Wants to continue to the PhD level and eventually teach in a management school
- Home town Longueuil, Quebec
- Single

Half way through her Master of Science program at Ecoles des Hautes Etudes Commerciales, Sylvie realized that what she really wanted to do was teach at the university level. So she changed direction and applied to the MBA Research program at Université du Québec à Montréal where she was given advanced standing.

"I wanted to have a more in-depth knowledge of my subject, and I like students. I like to teach because you are giving something to others, and there is always something to learn from the students," explains Sylvie.

In Sylvie's opinion, the strength of the MBA Research program lies in the high quality of its professors and the support it gives students to conduct paid research. In addition, second-year students are given an opportunity to teach and are paid by the course.

Compared to the Executive MBA, the MBA Research program is more specialized. However, it is still too general in Sylvie's opinion. A specialization is made up of three courses and a thesis. Sylvie would prefer five or six courses in the area of specialty.

Sylvie is hoping to do her PhD in either the United States or in Europe.

# Queen's University

- **INQUIRIES**

  Assistant Chairman
  MBA Program
  School of Business
  Queen's University
  Kingston, Ontario
  K7L 3N6
  (613) 545-2302

## FULL-TIME PROGRAM

- **APPLICATION DEADLINE DATE FOR ADMISSIONS**

  1 June (Advise writing the GMAT no later than March of the year
  for which admission is sought)
  1 May for non-residents

- **REQUIRED TO SUBMIT**

  - GMAT score
  - Official post-secondary transcripts
  - TOEFL score is required from candidates whose first language is
    not English
  - Personal statement (cover letter)
  - Résumé

- **AVERAGE GPA**

  3.3 or B+ or 75% (most emphasis on last two years)

- **AVERAGE GMAT**

  610 (Range: 540–750)
  If the GMAT is written more than once, the most recent score is
  accepted

- **PREFERENCE GIVEN TO A FOUR-YEAR DEGREE OVER A THREE-YEAR DEGREE?**

  Yes

- **NUMBER OF APPLICANTS**

  750

- **SIZE OF INCOMING CLASS**

  101

- **AVERAGE AGE OF STUDENTS**

  27

- **PERCENTAGE OF CLASS THAT ARE WOMEN**

  26%

- **PERCENTAGE OF CLASS WITH FULL-TIME WORK EXPERIENCE**

  91% (Average length of work experience is three years)

- **DISTRIBUTION OF UNDERGRADUATE DEGREES**

  BSc 30%                    BA 30%
  BSc Engineering 23%
  Other Undergraduate (LLB, Nursing,
      Rehab., Therapy, Commerce) 17%

- **OTHER RELATED PROGRAMS**

  Diploma of Administrative Studies, Executive Program (non-credit, non-degree), Master of Industrial Relations, Master of Public Administration, Master of Urban and Regional Planning, and PhD in Business

Queen's niche is that of a general management program. According to Tom Anger, Assistant Chair, "Its strategy is to be all things to all people. The administration at Queen's believes that its mandate is to teach the skills necessary to be a good general manager and therefore they feel they have to be good across the board."

The MBA program shares Queen's well-respected reputation. Queen's is a long-standing, established, and conservative university. Its image is not flashy but that of a school offering a solid education.

A concern among some students is that the MBA graduates are not marketed well enough to employers. This may be because the MBA graduates are overshadowed by the Bachelor of Commerce students. Queen's has an excellent commerce program, perceived by many recruiters as being among the best in Canada. MBA students and Commerce students share approximately six specialized second-year classes. However, with the employer's increasing emphasis on prior work experience, the MBA students are differentiated from the Commerce students and better qualified for potential employers.

The MBA program at Queen's is more quantitative than qualitative in nature, similar to those at the University of Toronto, the University of British Columbia, and McMaster University. During the admission process, grades in math courses are specifically evaluated. There is a good possibility that the admissions committee would question low grades in these courses.

The quantitative score on the GMAT is also important. If the candidate has not taken any math or stats courses and the nature of their work is not quantitative, a lot of emphasis will be placed on the quantitative section of the GMAT. Statistics is a mandatory requirement for admission and individuals without a university statistics course are required to take it as a condition of their acceptance. Preparatory work in calculus may be useful.

In September 1992, Queen's University is restructuring the first year of its MBA program. A modular structure will replace the two thirteen-week terms. Four five-week course modules and five compulsory one-week skill development modules will provide integration and co-ordination of the curriculum and develop individual skills. The second year of the program will remain in semester format.

Starting in the admission cycle for September 1992, more emphasis than previously given will be placed on the personal statement. It will be used as a check on writing skills and to determine if the candidate's expectation of the program is realistic.

For those people who are hoping to work overseas after graduation, Queen's participates in exchange programs with Japan, Finland, Belgium, France, Germany, and Indonesia. An agreement with the Moscow Financial Institute has been negotiated, and an exchange program with Thailand is in the process of being arranged. Approximately twelve to fifteen second-year students are accepted each year to participate in the exchange programs. George Kneisel, MBA '91, who exchanged with a university in Belgium, comments, "It opened up whole new vistas since I'm trying to get a job overseas." George explains that it was a perfect opportunity for him to start making connections while he was there.

Interaction with business is emphasised within the Queen's MBA program. As part of the International Business course, some students went to Moscow for a week to do research for their presentation. Students are required to travel, visit companies, and study on-site problems and solutions. This tends to minimize Queen's isolated geographic location. In one independent study, sponsored by the Department of Indian and Northern Affairs, a group of students went to one of the many poverty-stricken Native bands in Northern Manitoba with the aim of finding ways the Natives could become more self-sufficient.

## PART-TIME PROGRAM

■ SIZE OF INCOMING CLASS
6

To attend Queen's MBA program you must step out of the workforce. The part-time program at Queen's is almost non-existent because of the limited flexibility of the structure. There are only two or three elective courses offered in the evening. This may make it difficult for some employees to hold a full-time position while they are away from work for half of a day two days a week. The maximum time limit for completion is four years. This works out on average to be two courses per term, although some students take fewer and enrol full-time in their last year.

## PLACEMENT

The School of Business has its own placement co-ordinator who directs employment activities within the School for MBA and Bachelor of Commerce students. The Placement Co-ordinator also counsels on career options and job search strategies. This office is responsible for producing the annual *MBA Resume Book* and maintains statistics on employment of past graduates. Reference materials on corporations and corporate recruiters as well as information on School of Business alumni and the Queen's Business Clubs are also available.

Queen's Career Planning and Placement centre (CP&P) co-ordinates on-campus interviews and job postings for all faculties at Queen's, including the School of Business. CP&P and AIESEC (Association Internationale des Etudiants en Sciences Economique et Commerciales), a student-run organization, host approximately seventy-five companies at the annual Careers Day. In addition CP&P complements the School of Business's counselling service by offering skill-building workshops in Résumé Writing, Preparing for Job Interviews, and the On-Campus Recruiting Process.

The top-five companies in terms of numbers of offers last year were

- Andersen Consulting
- IBM
- Toronto-Dominion Bank
- Northern Telecom Ltd.
- Procter & Gamble
- Unilever

## ON KINGSTON

Queen's University's campus is very compact with ivy-covered limestone buildings. Most students live, at most, a ten-minute walk from campus. Downtown is only a fifteen-minute walk, and a car is not necessary. Queen's prides itself on the fact that its MBA program is full-time with almost all courses offered during the day. Also because Kingston is at least a two-hour drive from any large centre, students don't leave the university surroundings or the city on weekends. As a result, a tremendous loyalty and camaraderie develops among the students. One student describes it as, "very contained. It's removed from other major cities so there isn't a mass exodus on weekends. There is a lot of socializing within the student body."

Kingston is a university town, home to Queen's University, the Royal Military College, and St. Lawrence College. Its economic base is predominantly made up of institutions (post-secondary schools, six penitentiaries, and several government offices), tourism, and some industry. The population of the city of Kingston is approximately 69,000, but because it is a university town it has more cultural and social activities and places than other small cities of similar sizes.

## STUDENT PROFILES

### DAVID STANTON
MBA '91

- Full-time student in the MBA program
- Three-year BA in Political Science from Wilfrid Laurier University in 1986
- Worked for the Royal Trust Corporation of Canada as a trust administrator and trust officer
- Returning to the Royal Trust to work after graduation
- Home town Kingston
- Single

David had applied to the undergraduate Commerce program at Queen's but had not been accepted so when he was accepted for the MBA program at

Queen's he was pleased. The Royal Trust approved the program and paid for David's tuition.

Coming into the program with work experience was very important to David. He could relate what he was taught in theory to his experiences at the Royal Trust. "Experience makes it all come together. If I hadn't had it, it would have just been more theory."

When asked what he liked most about Queen's MBA program, David speaks highly of the mixture of case and lecture methods and also the high quality of the professors.

Two professors who David says were exceptional in his opinion were John Nightingale, a Human Resources professor, and John Gordon, who taught Production. He enjoyed the way both of them got the students involved. "Ten minutes might go by where only the people in the class were talking and they (the professors) were just facilitating."

David participated in an exchange with the Institute Gestion de Rennes, Rennes, France. Four out of his five courses were taught in French and, although he was only conversationally fluent in French, he did not have any significant problems since there were no written assignments. Finals in every course were worth one hundred per cent of the course grade.

David observed the French ways and culture. He found "the French people more analytical and forthright. Arguing can be part of a normal conversation, and they don't expect people to agree with them all the time." Canadians are more ready to agree to avoid confrontation.

Has the MBA helped David? "Definitely, I've learned to be a better worker. The amount of work you have to do makes you become disciplined." One piece of advice — "You have to want it or else you won't be very successful."


*TRACEY WILKES*
MBA '91

- Full-time student in the MBA program
- Four-year Bachelor of Nursing Science (BNS) from Queen's University in 1987
- Pharmaceutical Representative based in Toronto for two years
- Looking for a job in marketing with a long-term goal of consulting
- Wants to use her health services background and develop an expertise in that niche
- Home town Aurora, Ontario
- Single

Western and Queen's Universities were Tracey's choices of MBA schools. She is glad she went to Queen's "based on what Queen's has to offer." She prefers Queen's first year, which is predominantly lecture-style. "At Western there would be no one telling you how to do your internal rate of return, etc." You would have to teach yourself because of the case method.

Tracey was very impressed with Queen's application process. "They just don't look at scores. I had a poor GMAT score but I applied anyway and got in." Tracey built a case for herself by sending excellent reference letters and an autobiographical letter stating why she wanted an MBA and what she had to offer.

The atmosphere at Queen's was another asset in Tracey's opinion. "There is an open door policy. The professors get to know us very well. They know your name and can carry out a conversation with you in the hall."

As far as where Queen's could improve? "More funds have to go into the marketing of the school — especially in finance." Western has an excellent reputation, and this is partly a result of the way they promote their program. Queen's does not market or promote their program as well. Therefore, recruiters are not as aware of the quality of MBA students in finance.

The MBA was a wise decision for Tracey. "I came in with no business courses. I looked at it as building my business knowledge base. It's changed the way I think. I read newspapers differently. I approach conversations differently. Ten years down the road it's really going to help me make big picture decisions. Doing that with just a nursing background would have been very difficult."

# Saint Mary's University

■ **INQUIRIES**

Director of Admissions
MBA Program
Saint Mary's University
Halifax, Nova Scotia
B3H 3C3
(902) 420-5414

## *FULL-TIME PROGRAM*

■ **APPLICATION DEADLINE DATE FOR ADMISSIONS**

1 June for September entry
Students are admitted on a revolving quarterly basis to enter the
program in January, May, July, or September

■ **REQUIRED TO SUBMIT**

- GMAT score
- Official post-secondary transcripts
- TOEFL score is required from candidates whose first language is
  not English
- Two reference letters (both or at least one to be from a current
  or former teacher)
- Any additional information that you feel may strengthen your
  case

■ **AVERAGE GPA**

3.0 or B or 70–75%

■ **AVERAGE GMAT**

570
If the GMAT is written more than once, the scores are averaged

- **PREFERENCE GIVEN TO A FOUR-YEAR DEGREE OVER A THREE-YEAR DEGREE?**

  No

- **NUMBER OF APPLICANTS**

  365

- **SIZE OF INCOMING CLASS**

  97

- **AVERAGE AGE OF STUDENTS**

  27

- **PERCENTAGE OF CLASS THAT ARE WOMEN**

  31%

- **PERCENTAGE OF CLASS WITH FULL-TIME WORK EXPERIENCE**

  59% (Average length of work experience is one year or more)

- **DISTRIBUTION OF UNDERGRADUATE DEGREES**

  | | |
  |---|---|
  | BA 32% | BSc Engineering 12% |
  | BSc 26% | Other Undergraduate 2% |
  | BComm 25% | |

- **GRADUATE DEGREES**

  3%

- **OTHER RELATED PROGRAMS**

  Diploma Program in Marketing and International Business for managers, professionals, and individual business owners and Executive MBA

The total student population at Saint Mary's University is 7,000. Although Saint Mary's may be overshadowed by the size and reputation of its neighbour Dalhousie University, half of the student body at Saint Mary's is registered in the commerce faculty (undergraduate and masters level). This is a significant factor since it affects the amount of resources allocated to the commerce faculty. Dr. Chan, Director of MBA Programs, compares other schools to Saint Mary's University and states that Saint Mary's University has the largest faculty of Commerce east of Montreal, and the MBA program itself is of equal size to Dalhousie and even larger in its part-time component. The MBA program at Saint Mary's started accepting students in 1973, and now there are over three hundred MBA alumni working across Canada and in many countries of the world.

Saint Mary's University can be characterized by its personal nature. The students echoed this sentiment. Constancio Nabuma, MBA '91, comments that, "The small size makes the program very personalized. The profs go out of their way to make sure you understand, which is especially important when you come from a different culture . . . I was expecting a lot of fierce competition, but they help each other." In first year, the class sizes are approximately thirty-five and decrease in second year to fifteen to twenty-five.

Out of the total sixty-three full-time faculty members, thirty are actively involved with graduate students through teaching or research. Also, several part-time instructors are drawn from the commercial sector in the Halifax Metro area.

Each year Saint Mary's University accepts a few applicants who do not have an undergraduate degree. Vincent Taubman is one example. By scoring close to the 90 percentile on the GMAT and a couple of courses at the undergraduate level, Vincent proved to the administration that he was a candidate worthy of admission. Vincent manages the Halifax branch at Canada Trust and works with people's wills and investments. Each year approximately three to five students are admitted without an undergraduate degree.

The MBA program at Saint Mary's University is a generalist one made up of twenty-two half courses/eleven full courses, with a mixture of teaching styles from lecture, case, project, and field work. Students can specialize, to a certain extent, in their second year where they have four half-credit electives; for example, three half courses are offered in entrepreneurship. Saint Mary's has a Small Business Development Centre, which provides support and consultation to small businesses and gives industrial exposure and practical experience to students.

Another area of specialization could be International Business, in which students can choose from four half courses. Saint Mary's is one of two universities in Nova Scotia to participate in establishing an MBA Program in Xiamen, China. As a result Saint Mary's professors now travel regularly to China to teach MBA courses. Several Saint Mary's professors are supervising PhD students from China as part of the Canadian China Management PhD Program, funded by the Canadian International Development Agency. Saint Mary's is also involved in a consortium of Canadian universities that train Eastern European managers.

Approximately fifteen to twenty per cent of the MBA student body at Saint Mary's University are international students from China, England, Hong

Kong, India, Indonesia, Jamaica, Japan, Nigeria, and Thailand, to name a few. Although the students interviewed commented on how personable the professors and administration were, they were concerned about the lack of support for foreign students in two areas: limited sources of funding for entering students and no organized work programs during the summer.

## PART-TIME PROGRAM

■ **NUMBER OF APPLICANTS**
54

■ **SIZE OF INCOMING CLASS**
14

■ **AVERAGE AGE OF STUDENTS**
28

The flexibility of the part-time program at Saint Mary's University is definitely a strength. Tuition costs are paid per course, registration can be mailed in, and there is no minimum course load. Students registered part-time have six years to complete their MBA. Part-time students are integrated with full-time students since the selection of courses can be made from either day or evening classes.

One student comments that, "Of all the mid-terms and finals, I think I have only written two at the scheduled time. They have made alternate arrangements. They've been open to that."

## PLACEMENT

Placement at Saint Mary's University is handled through the Canada Employment Centre (CEC) on-campus. A résumé book for the graduating MBA class is sent to 250–300 employers across Canada. A student employment representative is the liaison between the MBA students and the CEC.

The top-five companies in terms of numbers of offers last year were

- Bank of Nova Scotia
- Irving Oil
- Metropolitan Life
- Sobeys
- Royal Bank of Canada

## ON HALIFAX

Halifax is a capital city that has changed dramatically in the last ten years. The waterfront has been restored to a cobblestone, traffic-free journey into yesteryear except that the old warehouses are now filled with interesting boutiques, sidewalk cafés, and restaurants.

It is a university town without equal in Canada; home to seven post-secondary institutions — Dalhousie University, King's College University, Mt. St. Vincent University, Nova Scotia Institute of Technology (NSIT), Nova Scotia School of Art and Design, Saint Mary's University, and Technical University of Nova Scotia (TUNS). Saint Mary's campus is small and compact, with most of the MBA classes held in Loyola Hall, which can be accessed from the residences by a covered cat walk. Dalhousie's campus is a five-minute walk away, and downtown is a fifteen-minute walk, or you can catch one of the frequent buses you can be downtown in five minutes.

Accommodation off-campus is hard to find. It is advisable to come to Halifax in July or August to "house hunt" because in September hardly anything is left. Six hundred dollars a month for a two-bedroom apartment is fairly cheap accommodation. If you want to live in residence, there are quite a few places available. The city of Halifax has a maritime atmosphere with a great night life if you have the time and inclination.

### STUDENT PROFILES

*KAY RAMSAY*
MBA '91

- Full-time student in the MBA program
- Four-year BBA from the University of Prince Edward Island in 1987
- Managed a retail clothing store for two years
- Short-term goal is a position in consumer research or marketing
- Long-term goal is director of international division of marketing
- Home town O'Leary, Prince Edward Island
- Single

"I come from a small university, and I didn't want to go to a larger school with a highly competitive atmosphere," comments Kay. The calendar from Saint Mary's University describes it as "a small university but with big ideas," and this is what Kay wanted.

What does Saint Mary's University do best? Kay replies that the school "develops the individual student the best. It hasn't lost sight of their mandate to educate. The professors know you by name, and they teach you to deal realistically with others in a business environment."

Kay was part of the Saint Mary's winning team for the Canadian Management Accounting Competition. They defeated Dalhousie, the champion of the last four years. This year Saint Mary's also won the MBA competition on Canadian-Hong Kong trade.

Computer facilities at the school are excellent, Kay commented. There are several Macintoshes as well as IBM compatible machines and laser printers that are available for MBA students only. There are no access problems even during peak assignment deadlines.

In Kay's opinion a weakness of the school is that the bursary program is not funded adequately. Also she feels that Saint Mary's University should be "better recognized for the quality university it is." A phrase she has heard from Ontarians is "SMU? Where's that?" However, she also feels that "It doesn't matter what university you go to, it's how you perform in the interview."

What has the MBA done for Kay? "I've grown up. I was twenty-five when I went in. I've been challenged and stimulated. It teaches you that success is accomplishing all your tasks to the best of your abilities."


*VINCENT TAUBMAN*
MBA '93

- Part-time student in the MBA program
- No undergraduate degree
- Has always worked in the banking sector and now manages a branch of Canada Trust specializing in wills and investments
- Came to Canada from England in 1977. Home town Liverpool, England
- Married, with two children

"Saint Mary's sends out material to the bank and advertises opportunities for mature students in the MBA." Vincent took some courses to show he could do the work and wrote the GMAT.

Taking the program part-time is difficult for Vincent. For example, "It's hard on family life. I have two boys — one's in Beavers and one's in Cubs, and it's hard to be there when you've got homework to do. I missed the concert my son was in. You have to make family sacrifices. I couldn't do it if my wife didn't support me."

"If I had the option, I would go full-time to get it over quicker. Getting together with groups is just impossible sometimes. I have to set up conference calls."

On the positive side, "I have an income." The bank pays Vincent's tuition, and "They wouldn't let me go full-time at my level."

When asked if the MBA would help him in his career he responds, "It won't help me that much because of my level, but it will give me the experience of the program. It gives me more flexibility in the job market. I might like to teach at Saint Mary's or in England someday."

# University of Saskatchewan

- **INQUIRIES**

    Assistant Dean (Programs)
    College of Commerce
    University of Saskatchewan
    Saskatoon, Saskatchewan
    S7N 0W0
    (306) 966-4785

## FULL-TIME PROGRAM

- **APPLICATION DEADLINE DATE FOR ADMISSIONS**

    1 June

- **REQUIRED TO SUBMIT**

    - GMAT score
    - Official post-secondary transcripts
    - TOEFL score is required from candidates whose first language is not English
    - Reference letters

- **AVERAGE GPA**

    3.2 or B+ or 75%

- **AVERAGE GMAT**

    560
    If the GMAT is written more than once, the most recent score is used

- **PREFERENCE GIVEN TO A FOUR-YEAR DEGREE OVER A THREE-YEAR DEGREE?**

    A four-year degree is required

- **NUMBER OF APPLICANTS**

    128

■ **SIZE OF INCOMING CLASS**
  41

■ **AVERAGE AGE OF STUDENTS**
  27

■ **PERCENTAGE OF CLASS THAT ARE WOMEN**
  30%

■ **PERCENTAGE OF CLASS WITH FULL-TIME WORK EXPERIENCE**
  65% (Average length of work experience is four years)

■ **DISTRIBUTION OF UNDERGRADUATE DEGREES**

| | |
|---|---|
| BComm 30% | BA English 11% |
| BSc 29% | Other Undergraduate 8% |
| BA Social Science 22% | |

■ **OTHER RELATED PROGRAMS**
  Master of Science in Accounting

The MBA program at the University of Saskatchewan primarily serves the needs of the Prairie provinces. It is a small program with a generalist focus, and the structure of the program does not include formal concentrations.

A niche that the MBA program at the University of Saskatchewan is starting to develop is international business. Although only three courses are offered in this area, the faculty are experimenting with two very innovative, applied courses. Saskatchewan's economy, based on oil, gas, and agriculture, is predominantly export based. Approximately sixty per cent of Saskatchewan's production is exported, with the majority going to the Pacific Rim countries. This provides students with the opportunity to work on projects involving contact with companies overseas and supports the University of Saskatchewan's international direction.

This is the third year for the International Business Course on South-East Asia. The twelve students enrolled in the class are split into six groups of two and are matched with six manufacturing companies in Saskatchewan. The students travel to Malaysia, the Philippines, and Singapore, as company representatives, making contacts, promoting their product, and conducting market research. Upon their return, the students present a business plan and sectoral study to their company and faculty. Joint ventures and technical knowledge transfers have developed as a result of student findings from this course.

In 1990–91, the University of Saskatchewan introduced a course on Cross Cultural Management, combining theory and hands-on experience in the international area. Part of the course takes place at the University of Saskatchewan. Students take six weeks of classes in culture and how it affects business practices and forty hours of language study in conversational Japanese. After classes end in May, the course continues at Nanzan University in Nagoya, Japan. Further instruction in Japanese takes place in preparation for a four-week work internship. Funding for this course comes from the Asian Pacific Foundation and the Toyota Corporation. Currently, enrolment in this course is limited to ten students.

Doug Bicknell, the Assistant Dean (Programs), comments, "We are taking small steps toward addressing the gap between management and the engineering technology side of operations." Students within the business and engineering faculties founded the Business Engineering Development Association (BEDA) which initiated a management of technology case competition. The University of Saskatchewan has placed second for the two years the competition has run. BEDA has recently become a national association, and next year's competition will be hosted by the University of Ottawa.

## PART-TIME PROGRAM

■ NUMBER OF APPLICANTS
   63

■ SIZE OF INCOMING CLASS
   32

Part-time students enrolled in the MBA program at the University of Saskatchewan have a maximum time limit of five years to complete their program, but extensions to six years are a possibility. Also, part-time students are allowed to take a period of time off if they wish since there is no mandatory minimum course load. Day or evening classes are available for students, although most part-time students take classes in the evening.

## PLACEMENT

The Canada Employment Centre facilitates on-campus recruiting for all students at the University of Saskatchewan. The graduating MBA class is relatively small (twenty-five to thirty) and many graduates seek employment with firms who do not recruit on campus.

## ON SASKATOON

The campus of the University of Saskatchewan is gothic in appearance with old stone mason buildings giving an atmosphere of tradition. The downtown core is a fifteen- to twenty-minute walk, or a five-minute drive from campus. Housing off-campus is available and reasonable. Sadiqul Islam, MBA '91, who came from Bangladesh, comments, "I came on September 4 and classes started on September 6, but I got a place right away." The Saskatoon Field House is a recreation complex adjacent to the campus that houses nautilus equipment, tennis, and track and field. Students receive a number of free passes to the complex.

Saskatoon, often referred to as the city of bridges, "Is a city of 200,000 that offers a lot of amenities but has an agrarian home-town feeling where neighbours talk to each other and are social," describes Mike Rushby, MBA '91. The winter weather is cold, but it is a dry cold and predominantly sunny.

## STUDENT PROFILES

*SADIQUL ISLAM*
MBA '91

- Full-time student in the MBA program
- Three-year BComm from the University of Dhaka, Bangladesh in 1985; MComm from University of Dhaka, Bangladesh in 1986
- Taught in the department of Finance at the University of Dhaka
- Plans to return to the University of Dhaka to teach
- Home town Khulna, Bangladesh
- Married, with one child

"I saw the brochure for the University of Saskatchewan, but there was no personal contact between the university and me before I got there. Sometimes the choice of the university is not an optimal choice," mentions Sadiqul.

Sadiqul's area of interest is finance. Unfortunately he found the University of Saskatchewan lacking in this area. "When I selected the University of Saskatchewan the courses offered in the calendar were quite good, but they are not offered every year." The few courses offered in finance and the limited choice frustrated Sadiqul.

Due to the general nature of the MBA program at the University of

Saskatchewan, Sadiqul's courses covered a broad base of subjects. This gave Sadiqul the opportunity to be exposed to areas that he probably would not have taken otherwise. Sadiqul comments, "I expected more in terms of the overall program but I learned a lot."

The next step for Sadiqul is to pursue a PhD. Although Saskatchewan does not impose differential tuition fees for foreign students, the University of Saskatchewan does not offer a PhD program. Sadiqul is looking towards the United States as a possibility. In the States, some schools impose higher fees for foreign students, but they can be waived if a student meets high academic criteria.


## MONICA KREUGER
MBA '93

- Part-time student in the MBA program
- Four-year Honours BA in Sociology from the University of Saskatchewan in 1978
- Partner in a photographic processing and enlargement company, an ethnic dance company, and an information brokerage firm
- Intends to continue working in her small businesses
- Long-term goal is to have a law degree by the time she is fifty
- Home town Saskatoon
- Married, with four children

The flexibility of the system to accommodate people who are not full-time students is a strength of the program, in Monica's opinion. Classes offered during the day are offered during the evening the next year. Monica comments, "What courses they have, they give students access to."

Monica found the faculty were understanding of the demands placed on her by her work. She was allowed to reschedule assignments due to meetings with clients or travel commitments. When Monica had a baby during the Christmas exam period, the administration allowed her to write the exam at her leisure. "There is a lot more trust than at the undergraduate level," states Monica.

When this interview was conducted, Monica was preparing to leave for Japan to complete her Cross Cultural Management course. She was looking forward to making contacts overseas and curious about working in the Japanese culture.

"Japan is still very male-dominated, and there are five women in the course. All the men have been placed in the manufacturing area. Three of the women are in retail/wholesale, and two are in the bank. I'm not sure of their expectations," says Monica.

How to break into international markets when you are a small company and helping small businesses develop growth strategies are issues Monica would have liked to have had addressed. "There is a 'large company' focus in the MBA program and that is not the reality in Saskatchewan. There is not enough focus on small business," comments Monica.

Monica describes her experience in the MBA program as "incredible." "I have grown professionally and academically."

# Université de Sherbrooke

■ **INQUIRIES**

Programme MBA
Faculté d'administration
Université de Sherbrooke
2500 boulevard Université
Sherbrooke, Québec
J1K 2R1
(819) 821-7333

## CO-OP PROGRAM

■ **APPLICATION DEADLINE DATE FOR ADMISSIONS**
31 May

■ **REQUIRED TO SUBMIT**
- Official post-secondary transcripts
- Three reference letters
- Personal statement
- Personal interview

■ **AVERAGE GPA**
2.5 or B- or 65–70%

■ **AVERAGE GMAT**
Not required

■ **PREFERENCE GIVEN TO A FOUR-YEAR DEGREE OVER A THREE-YEAR DEGREE?**
No

■ **NUMBER OF APPLICANTS**
150

■ **SIZE OF INCOMING CLASS**
40

■ **AVERAGE AGE OF STUDENTS**
29

■ **PERCENTAGE OF CLASS THAT ARE WOMEN**
15–20%

■ **PERCENTAGE OF CLASS WITH FULL-TIME WORK EXPERIENCE**
98% (Average length of work experience is four years)
Two years of relevant work experience is required

■ **DISTRIBUTION OF UNDERGRADUATE DEGREES**

| | |
|---|---|
| BA 25% | BA Economics 20% |
| BSc Engineering 25% | LLB 5% |
| BBA/BComm 25% | Other Undergraduate 5% |

■ **OTHER RELATED PROGRAMS**
Diploma of Administrative Studies, Executive Program, and Master of Science in Business Administration

Business policy is the focus of the program at the Université de Sherbrooke. No concentrations are offered. If a specialization is desired, the Master of Science in Business Administration, also offered by the Université de Sherbrooke, would be the program better suited to meet that objective. Also no advanced standing is given.

The MBA program at the Université de Sherbrooke is offered in French only. Most of the texts that are used are in French, and students have the option to write exams in either English or French.

A balanced approach of lecture and case — theoretical and applied — is used within the program to direct students in the development of decision making, group dynamics, and communications skills. From the beginning, students are placed in groups, and their interaction is monitored by an outside consultant. In the second semester the groups are changed, and a new dynamic is established. Fernand Guerin, Director of the Co-op MBA Program, states strongly, "It is important that students learn to communicate and react to other people." Also working toward this goal, students take a course on oral and written communication in their third semester. At the end of the program, the students take three courses in business policy.

The Université de Sherbrooke offers the oldest Co-op MBA program in Canada — introduced in 1966. The program is twenty-eight months in duration ending in August. Two fifteen-week work-terms take place between first and second year and after the completion of all classes in May of the second year. Students are responsible for finding their own work placements.

The first year of the program consists of only required courses, but during the second year seven electives can be chosen from about fifteen courses. Students also have the option of an independent project.

An interview is part of the admission process for entry into the Co-op MBA program at the Université de Sherbrooke. Fernand Guerin states that he is looking for evidence of motivation, leadership, and a check of the candidate's expectations. "It is important that the candidate knows that the MBA concentrates on the specific skills and on business policy," comments Fernand Guerin. Approximately five or six candidates a year are rejected based on their interview related to their objectives.

Every year approximately two or three candidates are admitted to the MBA program without a university degree. A GMAT score of 550–600 is required, as well as excellent work experience showing significant achievements.

### PART-TIME PROGRAM

Only the first year of the program can be taken on a part-time basis. At the end of the first year, students can either graduate with a Diploma in Business Administration or apply to the regular Co-op MBA program. The requirements for entry into the Diploma program are the same as the Co-op MBA program except that an interview is not required. Students have eight to nine years to complete the Diploma program, and almost all courses are offered at night. The Diploma program started in 1981, and since then 120 students have graduated.

### PLACEMENT

A Canada Employment Centre is responsible for facilitating on-campus recruiting for all of the Université de Sherbrooke. However, most students make their contacts and get their jobs through their work placements.

## ON SHERBROOKE

Sherbrooke is a quiet city surrounded by countryside. The pace is less hectic than in the nearby city of Montreal which is about an hour and a half away. Cross-country skiing enthusiasts might appreciate the availability of ski trails within a five-minute drive. For down-hill skiers, the University is located near mountains. The atmosphere of the town is friendly, and approximately thirty to forty per cent of the population is anglophone.

The campus of the Université de Sherbrooke is a fifteen- to twenty-minute bus ride from downtown, and the bus system is excellent. Around the university, accommodation is available and reasonable. On-campus, there are a number of activities including Friday-night pubs, volleyball, a theatre on-campus, and seasonal carnivals to name a few. One student mentions that there were lots of things to do, but that students enrolled in the MBA program did not have much time to participate.

## STUDENT PROFILES

### HELENE BOISSINOT
MBA '90

- Full-time student in the Co-op MBA Program
- Three-year BSc in Computer Science from the Université Laval in 1984
- Worked as a computer analyst with the Provincial Government
- Returning to the Provincial Government as a computer analyst, but working more with administrative projects
- Long-term goal is to work in consulting
- Home town Quebec City
- Married, with an infant

The Provincial Government gave Hélène an unpaid leave of absence to return to school to get her MBA. They agreed to pay for Hélène's tuition with the understanding that, if Hélène did not return to work for the Provincial Government, she would have to reimburse them.

Hélène took classes with students from the United States, Senegal, and Tunisia. The small size of the program allowed for frequent class discussions. Hélène comments, "It was important to know people's opinions from different countries — to learn their customs and how they approached problems differently."

For Hélène's two work placements, she worked in the information systems department at the Université de Sherbrooke and for a Consulting Group in Montreal. "I learned the importance of diplomacy. Sometimes the problem is not the design of the system," comments Hélène, "sometimes it is how the organization is using it."

Although Hélène had some excellent professors, "Some professors liked to teach to people who specialized in their area whereas most of the people in the MBA had little background in these areas."

If Hélène had it to do over again she would still take her MBA. "I studied computing science as an undergraduate, and it was very technical. When I worked with the government I worked with marketing people, but there was something missing when I tried to understand their point of view. The MBA gave me a more global view and better understanding."


*CLAUDE HARVEY*
MBA '90

- Full-time student in the Co-op MBA program
- Five-year BSc in Mechanical Engineering (Co-op) from the Université de Sherbrooke in 1986
- Worked for two years as a mechanical engineer in machine design for a small Japanese company in Sherbrooke
- Presently the Director of Production (sub-contractors) for Waterville T.G.
- Home town Sherbrooke
- Single during the MBA program, married shortly after graduation

Claude knew he wanted to do an MBA, but was uncertain as to the timing. However, two years into his job, it became more project management. "Since I was single and had no financial responsibilities, I decided to do it then," explains Claude.

One of the reasons Claude chose Sherbrooke's MBA program was because it was co-op. Claude comments, "You can see things the way they are done in real life. Sometimes in school it is very theoretical, but when I was at work I could understand why I was taught that, or realize that there wasn't such a good fit between what they taught me and what works."

Claude noticed a difference between the students that had had a work placement and those who had not. "When you come back you ask questions that are different because of the feedback you have had from the workplace."

In Claude's opinion, the MBA program could improve by teaching students how to give effective oral presentations and by giving them more opportunities to make presentations in front of the class. "When I was on the team for the Concordia Case competition, I felt there was something missing during the training," comments Claude. The Université de Sherbrooke's case team finished second in their division that year.

Claude believes the MBA has helped him, and if he had to do it over again he would. "After five to six years you are not doing engineering any more. You have to manage people and financial budgets. I'm using ten to twenty per cent of what I learned but I know it's not wasted. Maybe two to three years from now I will be able to use more."

# Simon Fraser University

- **INQUIRIES**

  The Director
  MBA Program
  Faculty of Business Administration
  Simon Fraser University
  Burnaby, British Columbia
  V5A 1S6
  (604) 291-3639

## FULL-TIME PROGRAM

- **APPLICATION DEADLINE DATE FOR ADMISSIONS**

  1 April but applications are accepted all year round

- **REQUIRED TO SUBMIT**

  - GMAT score
  - Official post-secondary transcripts
  - TOEFL score is required from candidates whose first language is not English
  - Three reference letters
  - Two applications forms (one to Graduate Studies and one supplementary application form)

- **AVERAGE GPA**

  3.4 or B+ or 78%

- **AVERAGE GMAT**

  580
  If the GMAT is written more than once, the scores are not averaged

- **PREFERENCE GIVEN TO A FOUR-YEAR DEGREE OVER A THREE-YEAR DEGREE?**

  Not necessarily

■ **NUMBER OF APPLICANTS**
   300

■ **SIZE OF INCOMING CLASS**
   50 (25 at the 500-level and 25 at the 800-level)

■ **AVERAGE AGE OF STUDENTS**
   27

■ **PERCENTAGE OF CLASS THAT ARE WOMEN**
   20%

■ **PERCENTAGE OF CLASS WITH FULL-TIME WORK EXPERIENCE**
   15–20% (Average length of work experience is two to three years)

■ **DISTRIBUTION OF UNDERGRADUATE DEGREES**

| | |
|---|---|
| BBA 30% | BA Political Science 8% |
| BA Economics 18% | BSc Forestry 6% |
| BSc Engineering 15% | BSc Math and Physics 6% |
| BSc Biology 12% | BSc Geology 5% |

■ **OTHER RELATED PROGRAMS**
   Executive MBA for experienced managers, a joint PhD program with the Department of Economics, and hoping to implement an MBA/Master of Resource Management in September 1992

"Rather than the traditional wide-ranging 'survey' approach to business studies, our MBA Program fosters the development of a specific expertise." This is how Aidan Vining, Director of Graduate Programs, describes the MBA program at Simon Fraser University in the faculty calendar. Vining comments, "The program is half way between a Master of Science and a Master of Business Administration because you must have an area of concentration." Students can concentrate their studies in Accounting, Finance, Management Science and Information Systems, Marketing, Organizational Behaviour/ Human Resource Management, and Policy Analysis.

There are two ways to enter the program. If a candidate has a Bachelor of Commerce or Bachelor of Business Administration, the student enters directly at the 800-level. Students take three to four courses in their area of concentration, supporting courses, and the choice of either a project or thesis. Completion of the program will take approximately two to three semesters depending on the completion of the project or thesis.

If a candidate does not have a Bachelor of Commerce or Bachelor of

Business Administration, their academic background must allow them to have the potential to concentrate — for example, computing or economics majors might specialize in management information science; math majors may choose finance; and psychology majors might concentrate in organizational behaviour.

Students with a non-business academic background enter at the 500-level of courses. It takes two years to complete the program. The first-year (500-level) courses are management skill courses and in the second year (800-level) you declare an area of concentration and specialize. In the Simon Fraser calendar, Vining says, "Your program will be custom-made, reflecting your interests and your goals; we have no MBA assembly line." Class sizes are small, and courses can be taken in other faculties such as Computing Science, Criminology, Economics, Engineering Science, or Resource Management.

Simon Fraser University's MBA program is one that attracts students with little or no work experience. "People who wish to specialize tend to go right through," Vining comments. Financial support is available in the form of a significant number of teaching assistantships as well as fifteen to twenty graduate scholarships, which average about $3685 per semester.

Tuition fees at Simon Fraser are comparatively low compared to other Canadian schools. For international students they are especially attractive since the same fee schedule applies to both Canadian and International students.

This may account for the fact that half the student body come from diverse international backgrounds representing France, Hong Kong, India, Japan, Norway, the United States, and other countries. The Canadian representation is mostly from British Columbia, with the rest of Canada under-represented.

An informal agreement that allows students to study for one semester at the Manchester Business School in England and the Helsinki School of Business in Finland is in place.

## PART-TIME PROGRAM

Technically there is no part-time program offered at Simon Fraser University, although it is possible to take a lighter course load at the 800-level.

## PLACEMENT

Graduates from Simon Fraser University's MBA program tend to get more specialized positions reflecting the nature of the program. Some students may be employed as financial or marketing analysts or staff specialists, while others may proceed to doctoral studies and university teaching.

The MBA program does not have an in-house placement service. The Canada Employment Centre offers assistance to all Simon Fraser's students. Neil Simpson, MBA '91, comments on job search support: "It's available but they don't push it on you. They don't go out and find jobs for you. You have to take the initiative."

## ON BURNABY

Simon Fraser University's campus is situated atop Burnaby Mountain, offering a breath-taking view of the surrounding mountains, inlets, and the city of Vancouver. The university, opened in 1965, boasts award-winning architecture. Beside the campus is Burnaby Mountain Park, which proudly displays several Native totem poles and offers serene trails. Burnaby is to the east of Vancouver. The trip down the mountain to downtown Vancouver, by car during rush hour, would take approximately three quarters of an hour. Regular bus service is also available.

The business faculty have three separate computing labs that adequately serve the needs of both BBA and MBA students. However, according to Neil Simpson, MBA '91, study space is a problem. Lounges have been taken over for office space. A new Business Administration building is planned for 1993.

## STUDENT PROFILES

*NEIL SIMPSON*
MBA '91

- Full-time student in the MBA program
- Four-year BBA from Simon Fraser University in 1990
- Looking for a position as a consultant in market research
- Home town Vancouver
- Single

Neil chose to do his MBA directly following his undergraduate degree because, "If I did not do it now I probably would not go back." Neil already had considerable work experience, and he was granted advance standing.

For twelve years between high school and university, Neil worked for an engineering company in ventilation controls.

A teaching assistantship helped Neil finance his MBA. He received $4800 for twelve to fifteen hours per week of tutorials, preparation, and office hours. To give him enough time for school Neil lightened his course load. He took two courses per semester with a project option.

Neil describes himself as being more on the quantitative side. Therefore, he particularly enjoyed learning analytical techniques and how to apply them. Neil also comments that "The limited enrolment provided a good relationship between students and professors and individual attention."

"A bit theoretical in focus," is how Neil describes the MBA program at Simon Fraser University. "I would have liked more real-world experiences and business-related items and less textbook."

To Neil, doing the MBA was definitely worthwhile. "It is a matter of getting more tools before entering the work force. It gives you that much more of an edge."

## CATHARINE WRIGHT
MBA '91

- Full-time student in the MBA program
- Four-year BBA from Simon Fraser University in 1990
- Targeting Human Resource management in Kamloops
- Home town Kamloops
- Married, with three children

Catharine gave up the position of Executive Directorship of a non-profit centre to return to do her Bachelor's degree. Her goal was a degree at the master level in Human Resources. She considered schools in the States until she discovered that Simon Fraser University offered a concentration in Human Resources.

The opportunity to finish her MBA in approximately a year, based on advanced standing, convinced her to chose Simon Fraser.

What does Catharine like about Simon Fraser University? "The strong theoretical orientation is something I enjoy." She goes on to say, "The professors are not just into research. Teaching and research is balanced at Simon Fraser."

Also, in Catharine's opinion, there is a strong focus on oral presentations. "In every class I had at least two oral presentations to make. I had an opportunity to practise and develop my skills."

Where could the school improve? "Since it is such a new program some administrative policies have to be worked out as can be expected —

particularly in the areas of orientation of new students and dissemination of information."

When asked if the MBA had helped her, Catharine responds, "Immensely. You tend to think you know everything. It is really humbling." However, she gives her husband all the credit. "He has been like a single parent with one income and three of us in post-secondary education."

# University of Toronto

■ **INQUIRIES**

Faculty of Management Studies
University of Toronto
246 Bloor Street West
Toronto, Ontario
M5S 1V4
(416) 978-3499

## FULL-TIME PROGRAM

■ **APPLICATION DEADLINE DATE FOR ADMISSIONS**
31 May

■ **REQUIRED TO SUBMIT**
- GMAT score
- Official post-secondary transcripts
- TOEFL score is required from candidates whose first language is not English
- Reference letters
- Personal statement
- Résumé
- Interview is recommended

■ **AVERAGE GPA**
3.0/4.0 or B+ or 75% (most emphasis on later years)

■ **AVERAGE GMAT**
580 (Range: 450–760)
If the GMAT is written more than once, the best score is used

■ **PREFERENCE GIVEN TO A FOUR-YEAR DEGREE OVER A THREE-YEAR DEGREE?**
Marginally

- **NUMBER OF APPLICANTS**
  500

- **SIZE OF INCOMING CLASS**
  100

- **AVERAGE AGE OF STUDENTS**
  29

- **PERCENTAGE OF CLASS THAT ARE WOMEN**
  47%

- **PERCENTAGE OF CLASS WITH FULL-TIME WORK EXPERIENCE**
  100% (Average length of work experience is five years)

- **DISTRIBUTION OF UNDERGRADUATE DEGREES**

  | | |
  |---|---|
  | BA Social Sciences 24% | BA Economics 12% |
  | BSc Life Sciences 20% | BComm 10% |
  | BA Humanities 16% | BSc Physical Sciences 4% |
  | BSc Engineering 14% | |

- **OTHER RELATED PROGRAMS**
  Executive MBA, MBA/LLB, MBA in Professional Accounting, and PhD

The University of Toronto's MBA school is targeting people with work experience. According to Doug Snetsinger, Director of the MBA Program, "We are seeking candidates with outstanding accomplishments. Typically, a candidate demonstrates these accomplishments in progression at work." Today one hundred per cent of the first-year class have an average of five years work experience.

Although math is not a requirement, and only suggested, the following is quoted from the University of Toronto MBA Calendar: "The Faculty strongly recommends, that entering students have a solid foundation in undergraduate-level mathematics. It is further recommended that their familiarity with that foundation be relatively current. Basic algebra is necessary, and advanced algebra and basic calculus are desirable." Needless to say that Toronto is one of the more analytical MBA programs. In Doug Snetsinger's opinion the admissions committee might question a low quantitative score on the GMAT, no quantitative courses at the undergraduate level, or a work history that is not quantitative in nature.

The biggest strength of the University of Toronto MBA program is its focus on finance. Fifty-eight per cent of grads last year were placed in finance positions, and the major banks were among University of Toronto's most active recruiters. There are no formal concentrations offered at the University of Toronto; however, students can choose their courses in such a way as to create their own concentrations.

If you are looking for an intense urban experience, Toronto's geographic location in the heart of the financial business community in Canada's largest city is the place to be. The program takes its fast pace from the community it is in, and because of its proximity there is no difficulty in getting top business people as speakers.

The building that the school of business is housed in at University of Toronto is old and tired. The interior decor is institutional with concrete block and narrow hallways painted yellow. Space is a highly valued commodity. Students have no viable student lounge; some classrooms lack audio-visual or technical facilities.

The University of Toronto is attempting to raise the money to build a new building through their "Breakthrough Campaign," in which they are targeting donations from the business community. This is part of their new and quite radical strategy of making their school of business market driven. Roger Wolff, Dean of the Faculty of Management, was quoted in the *Financial Post, Joint Venture Supplement* as saying, "One of the problems we've had with business education in Canada is that it's totally publicly funded. . . . Our goal is to move more aggressively toward a privatized operation. Private funding forces you to be far more accountable. . . . We have to make ourselves relevant" (27 Nov. 1989).

The image of a large impersonal institution that the University of Toronto has at the undergraduate level is not carried over to the Faculty of Management. A five-day orientation program is run the week before classes start. This is compulsory, and failure to attend disqualifies an admissions offer. The program is entirely run by second-year students. One student describes it as, "absolutely unbelievable how well organized it was. There was everything from an Olympia sports camp, to stock market games, tennis, canoeing, and drinking beer." Its purpose is both academic and social in orientation. The administration finds it especially helpful for international students who sometimes find it difficult to adapt to a new culture. Twenty-five per cent of the student body is from primarily Pacific Rim countries and Europe.

# PART-TIME PROGRAM

- **APPLICATION DEADLINE DATE FOR ADMISSIONS**
  31 October

- **AVERAGE GMAT**
  610 (Range is 450–740)

- **NUMBER OF APPLICANTS**
  500

- **SIZE OF INCOMING CLASS**
  50

- **DISTRIBUTION OF UNDERGRADUATE DEGREES**

| | |
|---|---|
| BSc Engineering 29% | BA Economics 10% |
| BComm 18% | BA Humanities 6% |
| BSc Life Science 17% | BA Social Sciences 5% |
| BSc Physical Sciences 15% | |

If you are committed to getting your degree quickly but do not want to give up your income, the University of Toronto has introduced the Part-Time Fast-Track program where students go through as a group. All of the students interviewed especially liked the camaraderie that was instilled in the fast-track program. David Littlejohn, MBA '91, describes it: "We were one class and stayed with the same class members for the first full cycle. It allowed us to get to know each other. My friends in other part-time programs said they felt like a number."

You are required to have a minimum of five-years work experience and take two courses per term, three terms a year. At this rate the MBA can be completed in three and one-third years.


## PLACEMENT

The University of Toronto employs a full-time placement officer to attract businesses to recruit University of Toronto's MBA graduates and facilitate on-campus recruiting. Placement is most helpful for students who have little work experience and want entry-level jobs. It may not be as helpful for older students with more experience and higher expectations. As one student mentions, "I'm not sure how much use they [the placement people] are going to be. I'm older and more experienced, and most positions that are posted are for entry level. Clearly, the program is designed for the majority of the students, and that isn't what I'm like. Fast-track part-time attracts older students. I know where I'm going. I know where I want to go."

The top-five companies in terms of numbers of offers last year were

- Andersen Consulting
- Royal Bank of Canada
- Toronto-Dominion Bank
- Northern Telecom Ltd.
- Global Strategy Financial Inc.

## ON TORONTO

The Faculty of Management Studies is in the heart of downtown Toronto. If you walk out the front door you are on Bloor Street amidst a very vibrant, exciting, and multicultural city. Within two miles of campus there are interesting neighbourhoods from Little Italy to Yorkville. A ten-minute ride on the subway will take you into the heart of the financial district on Bay Street, where you can go into the Toronto Stock Exchange and watch the action from the public gallery.

Toronto is an expensive city to live in, and housing is hard to come by. You would be advised to start your apartment search in the summer. St. George's graduate residence across the street from the school of business is cheap, but, as one student mentions, it has nothing else to recommend it.

## STUDENT PROFILES

*LEELAH DAWSON*
MBA '91

- Completed first-year courses on the fast-track part-time program and then switched to the full-time MBA program
- Four-year BA in Economics and Politics from the University of Toronto in 1981
- Worked for the past nine years with the Royal Bank in a range of positions
- Home town Ottawa
- Single

Having a full-time job in Toronto limited Leelah's choice of schools to either York or University of Toronto. "I lived closer to the University of

Toronto and I couldn't see myself going out to York at night on the bus. I don't have a car. Also, as an undergraduate, I had a good idea of what the University of Toronto was like — not the best school, but I knew I wouldn't have to compromise to get a good education by going there."

"I can't imagine anyone doing their MBA with kids. There were a lot of sacrifices to be made." For eighteen months Leelah was part of the part-time program. "I became more efficient with time. I learned how to not sacrifice your life to the program."

Leelah was at a point in her career with the Royal Bank where she was due for another promotion but having an MBA would be a definite advantage in getting the job she wanted. With the recession, she knew that a promotion would probably be delayed anyway so she decided to take a one-year leave of absence and finish her MBA full-time. While she was a part-time student the Royal Bank paid for her tuition and books.

Comparing full-time and part-time, Leelah definitely prefers full-time. "It is a very different pace. Part-time is more like a marathon and full-time is more like a sprint."

One of the highlights of Leelah's MBA has been the camaraderie within the fast-track part-time program. "Ten of us went to Mexico at the end of term whereas part-time students elsewhere describe their experience as being lonely."

An area where the University of Toronto's program could improve, in Leelah's opinion, might be the quality of professors teaching in the part-time program. "I've had some of the best teachers I've ever had and some of the worst. Most of the profs who teach the part-time program come from industry since most of the full-time profs have no desire to teach at night."

Has the MBA helped Leelah? "I have made life-long friends. It has given me a lot of ground rules to work from. I anticipate working with financial services, and I don't think you get the same kind of opportunities to think about as many businesses and commonalities and factors just through working."

*ROBERT RUTLEDGE*
MBA '91

- Full-time student in the MBA program
- Four-year BA in Economics/History from Trinity College, University of Toronto in 1982
- Seven years in the insurance business in pricing and marketing employee benefits

- Worked in Toronto and Southern California
- Can work in both Canada and the United States
- Targeting a position in strategic planning with a functional focus in marketing, finance, or MIS
- Long range goal is a position where he could manage a profit centre
- Home town San Diego, USA
- Single

Robert chose the University of Toronto because of its strong finance orientation. He had learned of the recent changes the school had made, including their modular program. Instead of taking a course for thirteen weeks, it was spread out — a week here, two or three weeks at other times — in an effort to integrate the material being taught.

He also chose University of Toronto for name recognition. "I have an interest in pursuing a career on an international basis and University of Toronto's name can take me beyond borders." Going to school part-time was never an option Robert considered seriously. He chose to do an MBA "because I was in a specialized business field, and I wasn't convinced I wanted to remain there for the rest of my life. An MBA was a tool that could change that."

To Robert, the University of Toronto's biggest strength by far is their finance program. The "profs in that area are excellent and are recognized internationally." Also teamwork at the University of Toronto is given more than lip service. It starts with the compulsory orientation where you are put into groups which you stay in for all of first term. "You all get the same grade, the benefits, and the problems. There is always conflict in a group. This is known and expected and something you have to deal with."

As far as weaknesses go, "The quality of teaching is inconsistent. Some is excellent and some is not."

On recruiting, Robert comments that the average age of people in the program is older now, and this is not ideal for recruitment. Most firms cater to twenty-three or twenty-four year olds with not too much work experience. "There is a conflict between what the available resources are and what the needs of the students are."

"Doing my MBA has helped me enormously, mostly because I did it for my own personal reasons: to develop a sounder business background and round it out. I'm ecstatic with where I am now compared to where I started."

# University of Western Ontario

■ **INQUIRIES**

Student Services — Admissions
Western Business School
Room 116
University of Western Ontario
London, Ontario
N6A 3K7
(519) 661-3212

## FULL-TIME PROGRAM

■ **APPLICATION DEADLINE DATE FOR ADMISSIONS**

15 May (Rolling Admissions)
Candidates are strongly encouraged to apply well before the deadline

■ **REQUIRED TO SUBMIT**

* GMAT score
* Two official post-secondary transcripts from each post-secondary institution attended
* TOEFL score is required from candidates whose first language is not English

■ **AVERAGE GPA**

3.2 or B+ or 75% (Range: B- and above)

■ **AVERAGE GMAT**

620 (Range: 450–770)
If the GMAT is written more than once, the most recent score is used
October and January dates for writing the GMAT are preferred

■ **PREFERENCE GIVEN TO A FOUR-YEAR DEGREE OVER A THREE-YEAR DEGREE?**

Yes

- **NUMBER OF APPLICANTS**
  1000

- **SIZE OF INCOMING CLASS**
  250 Full-time (No Part-time)

- **AVERAGE AGE OF STUDENTS**
  27 (Range: 22–50)

- **PERCENTAGE OF CLASS THAT ARE WOMEN**
  25%

- **PERCENTAGE OF CLASS WITH FULL-TIME WORK EXPERIENCE**
  99% (Average length of work experience is three and a half years)
  Ninety-nine per cent have at least one year
  Co-op work experience is considered on an individual basis

- **DISTRIBUTION OF UNDERGRADUATE DEGREES**
  BA Arts and Social Sciences 27%
  BSc Physical and Biological Sciences 17%
  BSc Engineering 26%
  BBA/BComm 25%
  LLB 2%

- **SPECIAL ADMISSIONS**
  3%

- **OTHER RELATED PROGRAMS**
  Executive MBA based in Mississauga, Joint Law/MBA, PhD

C.B. Johnston, long-standing Dean of the Western Business School, stepped down in June 1989 to return to teaching. Johnston filled the position of dean for eleven years compared to the five years that most deans stay in office. Johnston led the Business School during a period of considerable growth and was instrumental in the founding of Canada's National Centre for Management Research and Development at Western.

Johnston's successor as of 1 September 1990 was Adrian B. Ryans. Ryans had a distinguished record as a teacher, researcher, and manager during his career at the Western Business School. In 1987, Ryans accepted the Nabisco Brands Professorship in Marketing — the first member of the School's faculty to be appointed to a sponsored professorship. Ryans was also the Director of Executive Education at the Western Business School.

Western's press release on the appointment of Ryans states, "Ryans will step into the deanship in a period of financial crisis at most Ontario universities. The Western Business School will be severely impacted by a major budget cut that was recently announced by the University of Western Ontario." Ryans responds that, ". . . Canada deserves — in fact desperately needs — at least one world-class business school. With the help of our alumni and the business community, Western intends to be such a school."

As highlighted in the *Financial Post*, "The challenge for the successor will not be in building programs but in defending their school's stature. Some observers question whether Western can maintain the relevance of its case studies in a fast-changing business environment. Western officials say they are already preparing extensive new cases to reflect international business" (28 May 1990).

Western's Business School has an old and established history in Canada. The MBA program was established in 1948, and the PhD program in business was established at Western in 1961. The MBA program was modelled after the Harvard Business School, and in the early days most of the professors came from Harvard. The business faculty's long-standing history allows new graduates to call upon an extensive alumni network.

Western's MBA calendar describes its program as "tough, pragmatic and action oriented. It is not an academic exercise." Western prides itself on its practical orientation, and it supports this direction with the case method. The teaching style at the MBA school is unique within Canada. The case method is used extensively. At other schools the lecture method dominates first-year courses giving way to more cases in second year.

In the case method, the students are given about twenty pages of notes that set the basis for the objective or problem. The students read it over individually and come up with their analysis and recommended action. Within their groups they discuss and refine the case. When their class meets they are ready to discuss it. A significant per cent of the students' grades come from class participation.

The students have to take the responsibility for the learning. The professors are the facilitators. The case method recognizes the students' expertise and allows them to contribute their experiences to the learning of others in the class. Therefore, if your goal is to enter an MBA program directly upon graduating from an undergraduate program, the University of Western Ontario is not the school for you. Western rarely admits candidates without work experience.

The University of Western Ontario is often referred to as the number-one business school in Canada. Before applying, Lynne Sheridan, Director of The Business School's Student Affairs, has some valuable advice: "A lot of people apply to Western without thinking if it is the best school for them. They should come and sit in on a class to see if they like the case method." If you can picture a class of sixty very keen students trying to be heard, you can imagine that it takes an assertive, outgoing personality to succeed. In Sheridan's opinion, a good candidate would possess a well-developed sense of self-awareness, broad interests, and a high energy level.

The niche that Western occupies is one of general management with a global perspective. Students have the opportunity to spend one term in their second year abroad. The Exchange program was started in 1979, and exchanges are now offered with Denmark, England, France, Germany, Hong Kong, Italy, Japan, Netherlands, Singapore, Spain, and Sweden. Western's Centre for International Business Studies, active since 1974, is involved in research and case writing from which several international courses have been established. Funding for the Centre was partly provided by the Federal Department of External Affairs.

A new and timely course has been added to the curriculum — Managing Sustainable Development. Offered for the first time in the spring of 1990, the goal of the course is to develop more effective approaches to addressing environmental considerations in business decisions. Money to finance the course was provided by Dow Chemical Canada Inc. of Sarnia and Inco Limited of Toronto.

## PART-TIME PROGRAM

There is no part-time MBA program at the University of Western Ontario.

## PLACEMENT

Placement at the University of Western Ontario is facilitated by an in-house placement co-ordinator. Students are given guidance in career planning, searching for jobs, job appraisal, interview techniques, and résumé preparation. The Placement Office assists the MBA Student Association in the preparation of a placement booklet. The booklet contains the profiles and career interests of graduating MBAs and is distributed to over one thousand organizations within Canada and abroad.

Over two hundred companies advertise opportunities. The class of 1990 had an average salary of $49,800 and a range from $24,000–$120,000. The length of prior full-time work experience was probably a significant contributing factor. Information on the top-five recruiters was not available.

# ON LONDON

London's nickname, "The Forest City," hints at the quiet tree-lined streets that are home to the university. It has all the amenities that a larger city has but few of the problems. Western's campus is a ten-minute drive from downtown London. Most students have cars, and parking is cheap and accessible. Alternate forms of transportation are bicycle and bus. Housing is affordable, and there is a fair vacancy rate. One student comments that London was "great for jogging and not distracting for studying, but if I want a genuinely exciting weekend I'll go to Toronto." Another frequent comment was that the students did not get downtown very often.

## STUDENT PROFILES

### SANDRA BERETI
MBA '91

- Full-time student in the MBA program
- Four-year BAdmin from the University of Regina in 1984
- Worked at IBM for the five-year interval in marketing
- Targeting a consulting position or working internationally, perhaps in Germany
- Home town Regina
- Single

Sandra is part of the twenty-five per cent of the MBA students at Western that have an undergraduate degree in Business. Since her undergraduate degree had a predominantly theoretical base, Sandra chose Western's MBA program because she felt that a completely case-oriented program would benefit her.

Before deciding on Western, Sandra also considered European schools. She went with Western because "I thought I'd get just as good an education at Western, and it was more practical financially."

When asked if a Business undergraduate degree gave her an advantage, she replies, "The BAdmin gave me a short-term edge. I was more comfortable in the beginning because things seemed less foreign to me. It gave me a chance to focus more on the decision-making concepts." However, it didn't take long for the other students to catch up. Sandra did not receive any advance credits.

In Sandra's opinion the case approach develops a person's ability to think. "So many things are thrown at you. You have to be flexible. It is an excellent simulation of management: as close as you can get in an academic environment."

Western has one of the lowest men/women ratios in MBA schools in Canada. To Sandra, this had an effect. "There is not an equal influence because of the sheer numbers of men. It would be nice to have more female participation to balance things off a bit."

Western participates in academic exchange programs with other countries, and Sandra took part in an exchange with Germany. The school also has summer work programs abroad. Both of these are excellent vehicles for networking and exploring employment overseas.

Regarding Western's international focus, Sandra comments that, "Western is an excellent school, and it is starting to be international. It is slow because of financial constraints. . . . [An international focus] is a goal, but they are not going to sacrifice the core of the program."

Has the MBA helped Sandra? "Yes. I was in sales before, and you tend to centre on your own area. Now I think at a higher level."


## DETLEV NITSCH
MBA '91

- Full-time student in the MBA program
- No undergraduate degree
- Wide variety of work experiences from professional musician to private investigator to sales
- Targeting a consulting position, where his wide range of experiences would bring value to his clients, or a general management position
- Born in Germany, but grew up in Toronto and worked in Calgary
- Married, with two children

Approximately three per cent of Western's MBA student body is made up of people without undergraduate university degrees. Detlev falls into this special admission category. Throughout his career Detlev had been taking courses with the certified management accounting program. He completed his first year at Osgoode Hall Law School but had to withdraw due to financial constraints. He has also taken university courses in economics and computing science.

Detlev chose Western because it was the only school he knew that admitted students without a degree.

One of the best things about Western's program, in Detlev's opinion, is the case method. "The interactive discussion format is more useful for learning. You have to think about what you are going to say and be ready to challenge rather than just listen to lectures."

Detlev feels that the placement program is not very useful. The companies that come on-campus to recruit are "looking for someone who is going to sell their soul for the company and work their way up." Like other older students, Detlev is looking for a balance in his life that would include his family.

"I have learned a lot." In keeping with Western's generalist mandate Detlev comments that he has a broad base of knowledge, "fifteen miles wide and a micron deep."

# Wilfrid Laurier University

■ **INQUIRIES**

MBA Program Director
Wilfrid Laurier University
75 University Avenue West
Waterloo, Ontario
N2L 3C5
(519) 884-1970 extension 2544

## FULL-TIME PROGRAM

■ **APPLICATION DEADLINE DATE FOR ADMISSIONS**

Full-Time: 15 November
Note: Full-time program begins in May each year and continues
for twelve months of full-time study

■ **REQUIRED TO SUBMIT**

- GMAT score
- Official post-secondary transcripts
- TOEFL score is required from candidates whose first language is
  not English
- Two academic references
- One work reference from Supervisor
- Personal statement

■ **AVERAGE GPA**

78% final year (Minimum is 3.2 or B or 73% final year)

■ **AVERAGE GMAT**

614 (Minimum is 540)
If the GMAT is written more than once, the scores are not averaged

■ **PREFERENCE GIVEN TO A FOUR-YEAR DEGREE OVER A THREE-YEAR DEGREE?**

No

■ **NUMBER OF APPLICANTS**

120+

■ **SIZE OF INCOMING CLASS**

40

■ **AVERAGE AGE OF STUDENTS**

27

■ **PERCENTAGE OF CLASS THAT ARE WOMEN**

27%

■ **PERCENTAGE OF CLASS WITH FULL-TIME WORK EXPERIENCE**

100%

Work Experience is a requirement of the program. Fifty per cent have two years of full-time work experience or the equivalent obtained through co-op or internship programs. The administration accepts both co-op and internship programs (preferably sixteen months) as being the equivalent to two years of full-time work experience. If an applicant has less than sixteen months of work experience, then both the grade point average and GMAT score will become very important factors in the decision making process.

■ **DISTRIBUTION OF UNDERGRADUATE DEGREES**

BSc Engineering (The program is specifically marketed to schools who offer an engineering science, science, or math program) 80% Other Undergraduate 20%

Wilfrid Laurier University's MBA program is unique in many ways. It is one of the few MBA programs in Canada that is one year in length. The full-time program starts in May and continues for twelve months. The first year of other two-year programs gives people from diversified backgrounds basic quantitative and management skills, which they continue to build on in their second year. Wilfrid Laurier's program still requires this core but does not make it part of their program. Prerequisite courses in economics, management science, operations management, organizational behaviour, and statistics must be completed prior to starting the full-time program.

According to Gail Forsyth, MBA Co-ordinator, students enrolled in engineering programs can often pick up prerequisites for the full-time program through management options. For example, several students have completed the Engineering Management option at the University of Ottawa, or the Master of Science option at the University of Waterloo. Prerequisites can be taken at most universities. Students with a Bachelor of Commerce degree may have all the prerequisites already included in their undergraduate programs.

Most MBA programs encourage a student body with a wide range of undergraduate degrees. Wilfrid Laurier's full-time MBA has a technology orientation and targets people with technical or science backgrounds. The program does not give technological training but provides management skills. Originally the MBA was targeted towards the University of Waterloo's engineering co-op students, but in 1989 it started to recruit candidates from a variety of disciplines.

Bill Allen, MBA '91, who describes himself as a "non-technically oriented person even though I have a science undergraduate degree," comments that "I haven't found that they [the faculty] concentrate more on the technical end than I would like. There were technical courses I could have elected to take but I didn't." The part-time program came first and has been established for thirteen years, the full-time program is only five years old.

Three references are required as part of the admission process. Gail Forsyth comments that these "references are looked at closely."

MBA students at Wilfrid Laurier often get involved in projects initiated by the Research Centre for Management of New Technology (REMAT). "REMAT's mission is to aid the manufacturing sector in effectively implementing new technologies and to cope with change through a focus on tactics, implementation strategies, planning, problem solving, research, and training. REMAT invites faculty, students, and industries to make use of their database, consisting of over 1,000 annotated references dealing with issues and implications in implementing technology."

MBA students at Wilfrid Laurier also get involved in projects with companies active in international business and trade through Laurier Trade Development Centre (LTDC). "The LTDC was established in early 1988 as one arm of the Ontario Centre for International Business to enhance the global competitiveness of firms by assisting managers in developing trade-related strategies."

## PART-TIME PROGRAM

■ **APPLICATION DEADLINE DATE FOR ADMISSIONS**
   1 May

■ **APPLICATION DEADLINE DATE FOR PART-TIME EVENING**
   1 May (applicants writing the June GMAT will be considered only if space allows)

■ **NUMBER OF APPLICANTS**
   200+

■ **SIZE OF INCOMING CLASS**
   50

■ **AVERAGE AGE OF STUDENTS**
   32

There is a maximum time limit for part-time students to complete the MBA. Students take classes primarily during the evening from Monday to Thursday 7–10 p.m., although some part-time students elect to take the day courses that are for full-time students.

## PLACEMENT

Wilfrid Laurier University's Placement Office facilitates on-campus recruiting for approximately one to two hundred companies recruiting business students. Of these, thirty are recruiting MBA students. Among the top recruiters, in terms of numbers of offers given, were Andersen Consulting and Northern Telecom.

In Chris Deburgh's opinion, the administration is "very active in trying to get recruiters more aware of the program . . . and the profs promote the program with their industry contacts." However, Chris goes on to say, "The program is well known within a two-hundred-mile radius, but out of province people have never heard of it."

Most students find jobs on their own. To help students in their job search a compulsory seminar course is offered in the summer term. Speakers from the private sector are brought in, and instruction is offered on how to prepare effective résumés and improve interview skills.

The city of Waterloo is home to two universities: Wilfrid Laurier and Waterloo. The two campuses are within a five-minute walk of each other along University Avenue in the downtown sector of the city. Typical of university towns, it is very quiet in the summer when the undergraduate population leaves. This is an advantage for the MBA students who start their full-time program in May because they do not have to compete with undergraduate students in the housing market. In the summer, housing is plentiful. If you are starting your house hunt in September, however, you are advised to start looking early.

Students described the summer term as a time when you really get to know your classmates while on the MBA baseball team or at a barbecue. Mardi Witzel, MBA '91, comments, "It's no Toronto. It doesn't have the theatre and variety of things to do but, frankly, who has the time and money."

## STUDENT PROFILES

*CHRIS DEBURGH*
MBA '91

- Full-time student in the MBA program
- Four-year BSc in Chemical Engineering (Co-op) with an option in management science from the University of Waterloo in 1988
- Worked one year in material handling and one year as a process engineering supervisor in the automotive parts supplies industry
- Accepted a position with CP Rail Intermodal Freight Systems in their industrial marketing group
- Home town Leamington, Ontario
- Single

The one-year program was the selling point for Chris when he was deciding on which MBA program to apply to. The Wilfrid Laurier full-time program starts in April. "I would have had to figure out what to do with my summers if I had gone elsewhere," comments Chris.

The administration at Wilfrid Laurier recognized Chris's co-op experience and included it in his full-time work experience component. Also, his management science option at the undergraduate level met all the prerequisite courses required by Wilfrid Laurier's program. "Other schools would not have accepted them, or I might have had to write equivalency tests to gain advanced standing," comments Chris.

In Chris's opinion, one of the unique characteristics of Wilfrid Laurier's program is the marketing high technology course. For students who did not want this focus, he mentions that other marketing courses "provide an in-depth look at marketing tools in general. They make you critically evaluate models and techniques," says Chris.

"The MBA department and profs are very excited about the program," comments Chris. In particular, one professor that Chris will remember years from now, is John Banks who teaches Business Policy. "In my entire university career he is one of the best profs I've ever had." According to Chris, Professor Banks "brings out and directs discussion with an end where you learn something."

With a full-time enrolment of forty students, the program is small. To Chris this is an advantage because it facilitates small class sizes. He goes on to say, however, that the small size can also be a disadvantage because course selection is also smaller.

Has the MBA helped Chris? "Definitely. It has given me a different mind set . . . I can critically analyse situations, and it has improved my decision-making skills."


*MARDI WITZEL*
MBA '91

- Full-time student in the MBA program
- Four-year Honours BA in Politics from Queen's University in 1986
- Took most of her MBA prerequisite courses at the undergraduate level at Wilfrid Laurier University on a part-time basis
- Worked in advertising for four years with J. Walter Thompson in Toronto and Brighthouse Inc. in Kitchener
- Looking for a marketing position in the Kitchener-Waterloo area or a teaching position at the undergraduate level in a business school
- Home town Toronto
- Married, no children

"I am one of the few people who come from a definite arts background," states Mardi. Although the majority of students in the program have technical or science backgrounds, Mardi did not feel disadvantaged. "I've done very well in the quantitative courses. I have had to work hard, and it has paid off.

The professors don't expect a level of understanding that's above what I can do."

Mardi describes the MBA class as a small, very cohesive, and supportive group. She goes on to say that "Because it is relatively new, they [the administration] are really making an effort to get feedback." Two-hour focus groups are held every term in an effort to solicit suggestions of where they can improve. In Mardi's opinion, there is a very strong commitment to building a quality MBA program.

However, a program that is only five years old has its drawbacks too. Mardi comments that "Fewer recruiters come on-campus to recruit than at Western, York, or Queen's, for example."

Wilfrid Laurier participated in The Concordia National Case Competition in 1991 for the first time, and Mardi was on the team. Mardi describes the experience as "an intensive process. The ten-hour days were made up of preparing or presenting cases. It makes a three-hour exam seem like a cake-walk in comparison." Wilfrid Laurier University came in eighth out of eighteen. The winner was Memorial University, and Mardi proudly mentions that the Wilfrid Laurier team was the only team that beat Memorial in their round.

The MBA has given Mardi a broader knowledge base but also, she comments, "You learn about what you really enjoy doing in your spare time since you have so little of it."

One of the biggest lessons Mardi has learned was how to work in a team. "At first you want to do everything by yourself since you don't trust the others in your group but, because you have to do so much, you have to trust." Mardi adds that "This will be very valuable when I work for a company."

# University of Windsor

■ **INQUIRIES**

Faculty of Business Administration
University of Windsor
401 Sunset Avenue
Windsor, Ontario
N9B 3P4
(519) 253-4232

## FULL-TIME PROGRAM

■ **APPLICATION DEADLINE DATE FOR ADMISSIONS**

1 July

■ **REQUIRED TO SUBMIT**

- GMAT score
- Official post-secondary transcripts
- TOEFL score is required from candidates whose first language is not English
- Two reference letters
- Résumé

■ **AVERAGE GPA**

3.5 or B+ or 75% (most emphasis on last two years)

■ **AVERAGE GMAT**

560
If the GMAT is written more than once, the best score is used

■ **PREFERENCE GIVEN TO A FOUR-YEAR DEGREE OVER A THREE-YEAR DEGREE?**

No

- **NUMBER OF APPLICANTS**
  500

- **SIZE OF INCOMING CLASS**
  80

- **AVERAGE AGE OF STUDENTS**
  25

- **PERCENTAGE OF CLASS THAT ARE WOMEN**
  25%

- **DISTRIBUTION OF UNDERGRADUATE DEGREES**
  Honours BA 30%            General BSc 10%
  General BA 30%            Honours BSc 8%
  BSc Engineering 20%

- **GRADUATE DEGREES**
  3%

- **OTHER RELATED PROGRAMS**
  MBA/LLB

The focus of the Faculty of Administration at the University of Windsor is on general management. Students can choose their electives to form informal concentrations in the areas of Accounting, Administrative Studies, Business Policy and Strategy, Finance, Management Science, and Marketing. The option of a thesis or a major paper also exists.

The University of Windsor is in close proximity to the Ambassador Bridge, linking Windsor to America's industrial heartland — Detroit. The geographic location of Windsor presents students with a first-hand opportunity to study American business and supports the international perspective of the program. For overseas experience, students have the opportunity to participate in a work exchange program with France during the summer months.

An International Business concentration is expected to be offered in the near future. This program will consist of a series of international courses in the various functional fields, with a capstone course in International Strategy. Students in the International concentration will also take a Research Methods course with an international focus, or complete a major research paper on an international business management topic, under the guidance of a professor currently working in the field of International Business Management.

To be considered for admission to the MBA program at the University of

Windsor, applicants must have completed at least two semesters of university-level economics (introductory micro and macro) and at least one semester of university-level mathematics (algebra or calculus). Applicants who lack these prerequisites may be permitted to complete the appropriate undergraduate courses in their first semester.

Advanced standing directly into the final year of the MBA program may be granted to graduates from four-year honours programs in Commerce or Business Administration. Graduates from other four-year programs may be given advanced standing for these courses if they are equivalent to 500-level courses.

The size of the program is relatively small, by Ontario standards, and a strong sense of community exists among the students. Eric West, Dean, Faculty of Business Adminstration, states in the University of Windsor's MBA calendar that first-year courses are designed to permit the entering class to move through their courses as a team. Second-year courses provide students with substantial flexibility in designing their program of study.

In an attempt to attract women to the MBA program, the University of Windsor is offering two scholarships valued at $3,000 each for women entering the program. The admissions package states, "The scholarships are part of the University's renewed commitment to promote the enrolment of women in disciplines in which they have traditionally been under-represented."

## CO-OP PROGRAM

■ **APPLICATION DEADLINE FOR ADMISSION**
   1 May

■ **REQUIRED TO SUBMIT**
   A letter stating why the student wishes to be admitted to the co-op program is required in addition to the items listed under the full-time program

■ **NUMBER OF APPLICANTS**
   250

■ **SIZE OF INCOMING CLASS**
   24

■ **AVERAGE AGE OF STUDENTS**
   22

The University of Windsor is the third school in Canada to offer a Co-op MBA program. Windsor's first Co-op MBA class completed their degree requirements in December of 1990. Dana Tonus, MBA Co-op Co-ordinator, comments, "We are trying to attract the over-achiever. Eight months down the line, I have to place people. I'm looking for a calibre of people that I can market well. Co-op is not for everybody. It works for people who thrive on challenge." Part of the admission process for Co-op candidates is an interview. During the interview, leadership skills, motivation, enthusiasm, and communication skills are particularly looked for.

The Co-op program is twenty-eight months in length with a year of that period being full-time work experience. To give Co-op students the same course selection as regular MBA students, the four study terms coincide with normally scheduled class and term times. The three work-terms are sixteen weeks in length.

The calendar describes the process: "The first work placement immediately follows the completion of ten 500-level courses. The work placements provide the students with the opportunity to experiment with various areas of interest in a generalist capacity or to focus on a specific area of interest."

Work placements are not guaranteed. However, with a small enrolment, this has not presented a problem. Eighty per cent of the students were offered full-time employment by their work-placement employers.

In addition to the academic program, there is a compulsory set of twenty-one professional workshops on topics including conflict management, résumé and interview skills, and supervisory skills. In Tonus's opinion, Co-op students are getting "professional development over and above the academic theory." Aaron Smith, MBA '91 Co-op, found the workshops very helpful and mentions that "In the two months I have been working, I have found the skills you are being judged on are not just how well you can do a financial or marketing analysis, but your presentation, communication skills, and how you carry yourself."

## PART-TIME PROGRAM

■ **NUMBER OF APPLICANTS**
   100

■ **SIZE OF INCOMING CLASS**
   30

Students enroled part-time in the MBA Program at the University of Windsor have a maximum of six years to complete their program. Part-time students have the option of taking courses during the day or in the evening.


## PLACEMENT

On-campus recruiting is facilitated by the University of Windsor's Placement Centre. Other services they provide are workshops on how to prepare effective résumés and mock interviews. To augment on-campus recruiting a résumé book is published and distributed to businesses. The MBA Student Society organizes an annual "Job Fair" in Toronto for graduating MBA students to compensate for the isolated geographic location of Windsor in relation to the corporate headquarters of firms based in Toronto.

Co-op work placements are arranged through the MBA Co-op Co-ordinator.


## ON WINDSOR

The relationship between Windsor and Detroit is a combination of a "big town/small town." After a fifteen-minute drive from campus, you can be watching the Red Wings, the Detroit Lions, the Detroit Pistons, or attending the Detroit Philharmonic Orchestra and the Detroit Institute of Art. You can also enjoy the city night life and the restaurants in Greek town, Trappers Alley, and other culturally distinct quarters. At the same time, the quieter and slower-paced atmosphere of Windsor provides residents with the best of both worlds.

The campus is in the middle of a residential area and a twenty-minute walk from downtown. The architecture of the campus is a mix of historical buildings interspersed with modern ones. Housing off-campus is readily available, and there is graduate residence accommodation on-campus as well. Students have access to the University of Windsor's library facilities, as well as the library facilities at Wayne State University, the University of Michigan, and Michigan State — all within a half hour to an hour drive.

The city of Windsor is overshadowed by American media. The *Toronto Star* and the *Globe and Mail* are available as well as the *Detroit Press*, the *Financial Post*, and the *Wall Street Journal*.

# STUDENT PROFILES

*PEARL DAVIES*
MBA '94

- Part-time student in the MBA Program
- Four-year BComm from the University of Windsor in 1988
- Presently employed by Chrysler Canada as an Accounting Specialist
- Plans to stay with Chrysler Canada
- Home town Windsor
- Divorced, one child

Pearl was admitted directly into the final year of the MBA program because she had an undergraduate degree in Commerce with satisfactory standing. Comparing the two business degrees, Pearl comments, "The focus is different. You are doing a lot more research and getting into areas that are more current."

Pearl sees the MBA program at Windsor moving in the direction of global strategy.

The small class size and the interaction between students and professors is a major strength of the program, in Pearl's opinion. The professors are very accessible and so is the Dean of the Faculty of Administration.

Given a choice, Pearl would have preferred to have participated in the program on a full-time basis. "Going full-time is the better way to go if you can block off the time, and then you can get on with your life," states Pearl.

However, working and going to school on a part-time basis does have its advantages. By paying for their tuition, Pearl's employer encourages their employees to continue their education.

"I know the MBA will help me further my career since that is a criterion my employer will look at when deciding on advancement."

*AARON SMITH*
MBA '91

- Co-op student in the MBA program
- Four-year BSc in Biochemistry and Microbiology from the University of Toronto in 1988
- Accepted position as a Marketing Representative with IBM in their Kitchener office

- Home town Toronto
- Single

"I was coming from a totally non-business background, except for brief summer experiences, so Co-op really appealed to me. Combining work and academics would make up for what I was lacking," comments Aaron. Aaron is very pleased with the Co-op program at the University of Windsor and regards it as a "very valuable experience."

Aaron did his first and second work-placement with Price Waterhouse as a Financial Consultant in their Ottawa office. For his last work-term Aaron explored marketing with IBM in their Markham office. Aaron explains, "Co-op allowed me to look into various areas without feeling committed."

Aaron had no major complaints about the program. In terms of recruitment, Aaron mentions, "We had a good base of employers, but you wonder if it could improve."

# York University

■ **INQUIRIES**

Student Affairs Office
Faculty of Administrative Studies
York University
4700 Keele Street
North York, Ontario
M3J 1P3
(416) 736-5060

## FULL-TIME PROGRAM

■ **APPLICATION DEADLINE DATE FOR ADMISSIONS**

15 October for January entry
15 February for April entry
1 June for September entry
Advise taking the GMAT in the preceding January or March

■ **REQUIRED TO SUBMIT**

- GMAT score
- Official post-secondary transcripts
- TOEFL/MELT is required from candidates whose first language is not English
- Two reference letters (forms supplied)
- Supplementary admissions data form

■ **AVERAGE GPA**

3.0 or B or 70–75% on last two full years of study

■ **AVERAGE GMAT**

610
If the GMAT is written more than once, the best score is used

- **PREFERENCE GIVEN TO A FOUR-YEAR DEGREE OVER A THREE-YEAR DEGREE?**
  No

- **NUMBER OF APPLICANTS**
  Approximately 1200

- **SIZE OF INCOMING CLASS**
  280 in total [ 150 Fall – 50 International – 60 Winter – 20 Summer ]

- **AVERAGE AGE OF STUDENTS**
  27

- **PERCENTAGE OF CLASS THAT ARE WOMEN**
  30%

- **PERCENTAGE OF CLASS WITH FULL-TIME WORK EXPERIENCE**
  50% (41% have one to four years work experience; 11% have five or more years)

- **DISTRIBUTION OF UNDERGRADUATE DEGREES**

| | |
|---|---|
| BBA/BComm 35% | BA Arts/Humanities 14% |
| BSc Engineering 17% | BA Social Sciences 9% |
| BA Economics 17% | BSc 9% |

- **OTHER RELATED PROGRAMS**
  MBA with specializations in Entrepreneurial Studies, Arts and Media, International Business, and Real Property, MBA/LLB, Master of Public Administration, PhD

The Faculty of Administrative Studies (FAS) at York University is the largest graduate management school in Canada. FAS is able to offer students innovation in programming, flexibility, and diversity of choice at the elective level.

FAS was the first School to offer Arts and Media Administration as a special focus within the MBA degree. Arts and Media was introduced in 1968, one year after the founding of the traditional MBA. The program covers the fundamental and advanced skills and technique courses that are part of the conventional MBA core. In addition, the elective concentration in Arts and Media allows students to concentrate their studies on publicly supported, non-profit arts institutions, or on entrepreneurial arts and media activities in

Canada. An internship between the first and second year of the program gives students hands-on exposure to one of these sites.

Other areas of concentration within the MBA degree are International Business and Entrepreneurial Studies. The Fall of 1991 will see the introduction of Real Property as a concentration of elective offerings.

In 1990, FAS launched the first International MBA degree in Canada. The International MBA degree is a twenty-four month program designed to develop students with both international expertise and strong language skills to support the region of study. Fifty students will be admitted in the Fall of 1991. September is the only entry date into the program, and it must be done on a full-time basis. Entrance requirements for the conventional MBA must be met as well as proficiency in one of the foreign languages offered: French, German, Japanese, Mandarin, Russian, or Spanish. An oral proficiency exam is conducted at entrance and upon exit from the program.

Emphasis is put on proficiency in a foreign language because the student will be required to complete a three-month work internship abroad working in the language of that country. In addition to the work internship abroad, an academic exchange program at a foreign university is also possible. Courses in the chosen language will be taken throughout the degree. Instruction on culture has been integrated into the program to inform students on expected behaviour and customs of the country. The political structure, history, and economics of the region chosen is also addressed.

Lorne Schwartz, MBA '91, applied to the program "because of all the talk about globalization of business. The wall had just come down in Germany and Gorbachev was talking perestroika." He comments on his experience with the program. "It differentiates me from the other MBA students. There are only nineteen of us in Canada, and I emphasized this when I looked for a job."

Within the regular MBA, students can take international business electives as a concentration and are also eligible to apply for academic exchanges in their second year of study with schools in Brazil, China, France, Germany, Hong Kong, Italy, Japan, Korea, Mexico, Singapore, Spain, and Thailand. Within the country, a student can study at Laval University for either one semester or the joint York/Laval MBA Degree.

When Carol Pattenden, Admissions Officer, answers inquiries about the program, she often comes across prospective students who feel that they need higher grades and GMAT scores than the stated requirements of the program. "In reality," she says, "if you have a 580 GMAT score with an even split between quantitative and verbal, a solid B average on the last two full years of study, an undergraduate degree — three or four years — you have a good chance of being admitted."

The program is not strictly targeting people with full-time work experience. In fact, there is an even split in the full-time program between people directly from an undergraduate degree program and those with full-time work experience. The administration does not predict that this will change in the immediate future because there are many job opportunities still available for graduates without full-time work experience. However, if your grades or GMAT are marginal, the work-experience factor is a significant one.

Currently, York has an advanced standing policy. A candidate with a three-year degree can gain advanced standing for up to five of the twenty courses that make up the MBA. Candidates with either a four-year BBA or BComm degree can receive up to ten advanced standing credits. To qualify for exemptions, the equivalent course work must have been taken within the last five years. A qualifying exam may be required. This policy is now under review and may change in the future.

## PART-TIME PROGRAM

■ **NUMBER OF APPLICANTS**
Approximately 700

■ **SIZE OF INCOMING CLASS**
350 in total  [ 150 Fall  —  120 Winter  —  80 Summer ]

■ **AVERAGE AGE OF STUDENTS**
29

■ **DISTRIBUTION OF UNDERGRADUATE DEGREES**

| | |
|---|---|
| BBA/BComm 37% | BA Social Sciences 7% |
| BSc Engineering 24% | BA Arts/Humanities 6% |
| BSc 21% | BA Economics 5% |

There is a six-year maximum time limit for students to complete York's MBA program part-time. Students can take classes either at night or during the day, although most York part-time students choose to take their classes in the evening. Students pay per course.

Transferring from part-time to full-time and vice versa is easily done by informing the administration in advance. The ease in transferring, the tri-semester structure, the choice of day or night courses, and the size of the part-time program certainly characterize York's MBA program as flexible. In fact one student comments that York seems to "tailor education to your needs."

## PLACEMENT

York has an in-house student placement service that facilitates on-campus recruiting. In addition, a placement directory of résumés for both MBA and BBA graduates is published and sent to five hundred potential employers in both the private and public sector. Students have an opportunity to meet employers in September, before on-campus recruiting begins, by attending Career Day. Thirty-five major companies send representatives to answer students' questions and give out information on their companies.

Nancy Wallace, Manager of Placement Services, comments that "One of our biggest services is how we educate the student to become self-sufficient for life in job search techniques." Nancy was formerly a recruiter and head hunter. Her business background allows her to give a first-hand account of what some businesses are looking for.

The students interviewed feel that the placement service provided opportunities for those who were looking for entry-level positions. The Immediate Opening Service, which posts approximately three hundred positions, offers positions requiring no work experience to seven years of work experience. The Immediate Opening Service includes every kind of company and position, but the positions are available immediately. This service is most useful to students who are close to graduation.

The top-five companies in terms of numbers of offers last year were

- General Mills
- IBM
- Imperial Oil
- Royal Bank of Canada
- Toronto-Dominion Bank

## ON NORTH YORK

North York is part of Metropolitan Toronto, although to get to downtown Toronto by public transit it would take approximately one hour (even though the transit service is excellent), or a half hour by car depending on the traffic. York's campus is in the middle of a very busy traffic area, and one student describes the quality of life as "hectic."

The campus itself is very windy and barren of trees. A recent twenty-two million dollar building campaign was responsible for the addition of an academic building, student centre, student housing, and a commercial centre,

York Lanes. Housing is available on-campus for graduate students and is quite reasonable. Be advised however, that if you do want to live on-campus, you should start looking in June or July. A lot of second-year students living off-campus in the first year move on-campus in second year to minimize time wasted commuting.

Socially there are a lot of resources. The Metropolitan Track and Field Centre is right on-campus and is available to students. There are also lunch-time concerts, a bird sanctuary, and York's own art gallery.

## STUDENT PROFILES

### ANN CASTRO
MBA '91

- Full-time student in the MBA program
- Four-year BSc in Chemical Engineering from the University of Toronto in 1986
- Worked as an engineer in the pulp and paper and computing industries
- Accepted position as Associate with Solomon Brothers in Frankfurt, Germany
- Home town Duesseldorf, Germany
- Single

"I felt like I could be myself and that York's MBA program would bring out the best in me," explains Ann. Ann applied to York with below-average grades in her engineering degree, but "They were more interested in a well-rounded person than in perfect grades." The admissions people took into consideration Ann's international experience and her potential for achievement. "They took a chance on me; they treat people like people," comments Ann.

Admitting Ann was a good decision. Ann applied to only four companies for employment through on-campus recruiting, two of which decided not to recruit, and she received job offers from the other two. "People who aren't 'hot shots' can be achievers," states Ann.

In Ann's opinion, the students enrolled in the MBA program are a very close group with a high level of camaraderie. She attributes this to the orientation weekend that takes place after the first week of classes at a camp outside of Toronto. The retreat is organized by the students in the Graduate Business Council, and it has a purely non-academic, social emphasis. The orientation weekend is an optional event.

Ann had a number of professors from industry who contributed practical experience as well as theory. Two members of the faculty, who in Ann's opinion were excellent professors, were Brenda Zimmerman, who taught accounting and received a teaching award, and James Gillies, who taught policy and was Ann's advisor for "601." Ann describes them: "They were tough but fair, and they really tried to help students." Overall, Ann was very impressed with the professors at York's MBA program.

In Ann's first year, she applied for an exchange program with Spain. She felt that the communication between the administration operating the exchange and the subject areas could be better. Although she was accepted into the exchange program, she declined because of the frustration involved in the scheduling of her major project. Ann encourages people to apply for the exchange program, but emphasizes that planning ahead is important.

The MBA experience has definitely been a positive one for Ann. "I have really grown as a person and the program has changed me from a fairly average person into a winner."

## DAVID WEATHERSEED
MBA '90

- Part-time student in the MBA program
- Four-year BSc in Mechanical Engineering from the University of Western Ontario in 1983
- Worked in the material-handling industry as a field-sales engineer
- MBA tuition paid for by his employer
- Focused job search on "top 100" companies in sales and marketing areas
- Home town Toronto
- Married, with two children

"I enjoyed taking the program on a part-time basis," David comments. "It allowed me the time to really understand the importance of the material being taught." He goes on to say that "In addition to gaining the academic education from the program, I was also able to see the applications in the real world."

From David's PC at home, he was able to access the Faculty of Administration mainframe and YorkLine, York's Library catalogue service. The computer advisors at York were extremely helpful. They could be reached in person, over the phone, and on-line. The library's computing facilities at York are excellent in David's opinion.

The Outstanding Achievement Award for the best Policy 601 project was given to the group of which David was a member. "The project required applying knowledge from all of the areas studied, including understanding and development of the significant issues to the site. The project was successful because of the excellent group I was in and the input of the faculty advisors."

One common thread that was observed to be continuous throughout the program was the importance of strategy. "Everyone talked strategy. It was emphasized in the classroom, in the cases, and in group discussions."

This emphasis on strategy has had a tremendous affect on David. "It has caused me to rethink my career objectives. My attitude towards organization and management styles has changed since I first started the program." David has decided that he "works better with a more progressive management style. One that is strategic. The industry I was in did not grow as I did" and caused him to rethink his strategies.

David advises that students network with colleagues, teachers, and business associates. It is important to assist you in understanding the material better by balancing the education with different opinions. Also, "The MBA is as much social as it is academic. It takes a lot of dedication but is a lot of fun."

David describes the MBA as "a data base of knowledge that is learned over a period of time. It is a succinct way of learning different aspects of business, both theoretical and practical, from excellent teachers and is highly valuable in progressing my life."

# Major Trends

## NICHE MARKETING

The applicant pool is beginning to shrink as demographics show fewer people of the traditional age are applying to business schools. Also, the MBA has begun to lose its shine as the degree that will guarantee a great job with a high salary as the number of people with MBA's climb. Certainly the ratios of applicants to openings are still high, but a slight downturn has begun.

As a result of this, business schools are now in a position where they have to start pro-active recruiting. A trend towards niche marketing is beginning. Business schools are now actively trying to differentiate themselves from each other. However, in Canada this is still a very tentative beginning. A school will begin to specialize, but it does not want to let go of the old premise that it offers a general MBA. In the States, however, this trend is much more advanced.

## INCREASING AGE OF STUDENTS

Some universities, like Concordia University, Université Laval, University of Western Ontario, University of Toronto, and University of British Columbia are targeting applicants with three or more years of full-time managerial work experience. However, with the more mature student come higher expectations. Mature students want value for their dollars. "It is costing me $1,000 a day with loss of salary and earning potential. Did I get that value?" They have less tolerance for poor teaching, and they want practical courses, less rigid rules, and to be taught as an adult. Part-time students demand accessibility to administration during evening hours and better course selection in the evenings and intersession.

## INTERNATIONAL EMPHASIS

The last major overhaul of business-school curriculum was fifteen to twenty years ago when the business community was calling for more emphasis on small business. Courses were developed and institutes put into place.

Today MBA schools are placing the emphases on giving students a grounding in the issues surrounding international business. Free trade, the tearing down of the Berlin Wall, and the EEC Common Market of 1992 have added to the globalization of business. MBA schools are reacting to the need:

- York University has introduced an International Master of Business Administration and admitted its first formal class in September of 1991.

- The University of Ottawa/Université d'Ottawa introduced a new International Management stream in September of 1991.

- Both York University and the University of Ottawa/Université d'Ottawa have work placements abroad as part of the program requirements and a second language prerequisite.

- Universities on the coasts, especially University of British Columbia, Simon Fraser University, Dalhousie University, and Saint Mary's University, attract a large contingent of foreign students due to their location. McGill University also has a significant foreign student enrolment in spite of its geography.

MBA schools are reacting to the needs of business. However, they are not the leaders in this area. The need for managers with international experience and familiarization with how different cultures conduct business has been apparent for some time. Centres of International Business were established at selected universities across Canada as early as 1974. However, like any large organization, it takes time for MBA schools to make changes. This is compounded by the fact that schools of business have tenured professors with specific areas of expertise. The current issues concerning business today are ethics in business, the management of information, and the environment.


## THE SOFT SKILLS

Business is also asking MBA schools to graduate students with excellent communication and people skills. Demographics show that the bulge of the population, "the boomers," are now in their thirties and forties. The smaller "baby bust" generation, which will fill the entry-level positions, has brought corporations to realize that people are their most valuable resource.

- Ecole des Hautes Etudes Commerciales and the University of Western Ontario use a teaching style that is predominantly case-study to develop these skills in their students. The University of Calgary uses extensive project implementation.

- Memorial University of Newfoundland is making its mark as the school to beat in the Concordia National Case competition. Their case team came in first in 1991, 1990, and 1988; and came in second in 1989 to the University of Ottawa/Université d'Ottawa.

## TO BE ABLE TO HIT THE GROUND RUNNING

Co-op programs give students with little work experience the chance to try out different settings before committing themselves in the permanent job search. The majority of people in MBA programs are using the degree to act as a spring board for a career change. The Co-op program helps these people form a network in the new area they wish to enter.

The Co-op system is advantageous for employers in business because it gives them an opportunity to see a student's potential in their workplace before having to make a decision to hire them as a permanent employee. In a time of recession and budget cutbacks this is especially important.

There are only three universities in Canada that offer Co-op MBA programs — Université de Sherbrooke, McMaster University, and the University of Windsor. Sherbrooke established the first Co-op program in 1966, followed by McMaster in 1971 and Windsor in 1989.

# Comparative Statistics

*Note:* The following statistics are for the class of 1990–91. Be advised that business schools do not use a standard method of collecting data. For example, some schools take the average age of the applicants that were offered admission, whereas other schools take it on the basis of those who accepted the offer. Some schools round off to two significant figures, and others make their calculations to three. For the purposes of the following statistics, only two significant figures are used. These statistics are to be used only as a guide.

## PERCENTAGE OF WOMEN ENROLLED IN MBA PROGRAMS IN 1990–91*

| | | |
|---|---|---|
| Université de Sherbrooke | 18% | |
| Simon Fraser University | 20% | |
| University of Western Ontario | 25% | |
| University of Windsor | 25% | |
| Queen's University | 26% | |
| Wilfrid Laurier University | 27% | |
| University of British Columbia | 29% | |
| University of New Brunswick | 30% | |
| University of Saskatchewan | 30% | |
| York University | 30% | |
| Saint Mary's University | 31% | |
| University of Alberta | 32% | |
| University of Calgary | 33% | |
| University of Manitoba | 34% | |
| McGill University | 35% | |
| Concordia University | 37% | |
| Memorial University of Newfoundland | 37% | |
| McMaster University | 38% | |
| Dalhousie University | 40% | |
| Ecoles des Hautes Etudes Commerciales | 40% | |
| Université du Québec à Montréal | 40% | (Exec. MBA) |
| Laval University | 41% | |
| University of Toronto | 47% | |
| Université de Moncton | 50% | |
| University of Ottawa/Université d'Ottawa | 50% | |
| Université du Québec à Montréal | 57% | (MBA Research) |

* *Laurentian University/Université Laurentienne's statistics on % women not available*

## AVERAGE AGE OF STUDENTS IN
## FULL-TIME MBA PROGRAMS*

| | |
|---|---|
| Université de Moncton | 24 |
| McGill University | 25 |
| McMaster University | 25 |
| University of Ottawa/Université d'Ottawa | 25 |
| University of Windsor | 25 |
| University of British Columbia | 26 |
| Dalhousie University | 26 |
| Université du Québec à Montréal | 26 (MBA Research) |
| University of Alberta | 27 |
| Concordia University | 27 |
| Memorial University of Newfoundland | 27 |
| Queen's University | 27 |
| Saint Mary's University | 27 |
| University of Saskatchewan | 27 |
| Simon Fraser University | 27 |
| University of Western Ontario | 27 |
| Wilfrid Laurier University | 27 |
| York University | 27 |
| University of Manitoba | 28 |
| University of New Brunswick | 28 |
| Université Laval | 29 |
| Université de Sherbrooke | 29 |
| University of Toronto | 29 |
| Ecoles des Hautes Etudes Commerciales | 30 |
| University of Calgary | 31 |
| Université du Québec à Montréal | 37 (Exec. MBA) |

---

* *Laurentian University/Université Laurentienne's statistics on average age not available*

# RATIO OF APPLICATIONS TO ACCEPTANCES FOR FULL-TIME MBA PROGRAMS BY UNIVERSITY*

*University / Number of applications to acceptances / Ratio of applications to acceptances*

| University | Number of applications to acceptances | Ratio of applications to acceptances |
|---|---|---|
| Université de Moncton | 45 : 30 | 1.5 : 1 |
| Université du Québec à Montréal (MBA Research) | 219 : 102 | 2.1 : 1 |
| University of New Brunswick | 80 : 30 | 2.7 : 1 |
| Université du Québec à Montréal (Exec. MBA) | 400 : 15 | 02.7 : 1 |
| Wilfrid Laurier University | 120 : 40 | 3.0 : 1 |
| University of Saskatchewan | 128 : 41 | 3.1 : 1 |
| Université Laval | 183 : 57 | 3.2 : 1 |
| Saint Mary's University | 365 : 97 | 3.8 : 1 |
| Université de Sherbrooke | 150 : 40 | 3.8 : 1 |
| University of Western Ontario | 1000 : 250 | 4.0 : 1 |
| York University | 1200 : 280 | 4.3 : 1 |
| McMaster University | 303 : 68 | 4.5 : 1 |
| University of Toronto | 500 : 100 | 5.0 : 1 |
| University of Manitoba | 208 : 39 | 5.3 : 1 |
| University of British Columbia *(after rigorous pre-screening)* | 780 : 144 | 5.4 : 1 |
| Memorial University of Newfoundland | 83 : 15 | 5.5 : 1 |
| University of Ottawa/Université d'Ottawa | 494 : 90 | 5.5 : 1 |
| Dalhousie University | 600 : 100 | 6.0 : 1 |
| Simon Fraser University | 300 : 50 | 6.0 : 1 |
| Concordia University | 531 : 87 | 6.1 : 1 |
| University of Windsor | 500 : 80 | 6.3 : 1 |
| University of Calgary | 420 : 60 | 7.0 : 1 |
| Queen's University | 750 : 101 | 7.4 : 1 |
| McGill University | 900 : 120 | 7.5 : 1 |
| University of Alberta | 284 : 31 | 9.2 : 1 |
| Ecoles des Hautes Etudes Commerciales | 573 : 54 | 10.6 : 1 |

* *Laurentian University/Université Laurentienne's does not offer a full-time program*

# RATIO OF APPLICATIONS TO ACCEPTANCES
# FOR PART-TIME MBA PROGRAMS*

*University  /  Number of applications to acceptances  /  Ratio of applications to acceptances*

| | | |
|---|---|---|
| University of Alberta | 52 : 47 | 1.1 : 1 |
| University of New Brunswick | 60 : 45 | 1.3 : 1 |
| Memorial University of Newfoundland | 61 : 40 | 1.5 : 1 |
| Université de Moncton | 45 : 30 | 1.5 : 1 |
| McMaster University | 136 : 68 | 2.0 : 1 |
| University of Saskatchewan | 63 : 32 | 2.0 : 1 |
| York University *(approx.)* | 700 : 350 | 2.0 : 1 |
| University of British Columbia *(after rigorous pre-screening)* | 94 : 45 | 2.1 : 1 |
| University of Ottawa/Université d'Ottawa | 295 : 132 | 2.2 : 1 |
| University of Manitoba | 95 : 41 | 2.3 : 1 |
| University of Windsor | 100 : 30 | 3.3 : 1 |
| Concordia University | 336 : 89 | 3.8 : 1 |
| Saint Mary's University | 54 : 14 | 3.9 : 1 |
| McGill University | 600 : 150 | 4.0 : 1 |
| Wilfrid Laurier University | 200 : 50 | 4.0 : 1 |
| University of Toronto | 500 : 50 | 10.0 : 1 |

* *Data not available for University of Calgary, Dalhousie University, Ecoles des Hautes Etudes Commerciales, Laurentian University/Université Laurentienne, Laval University, or Université du Québec à Montréal. Queen's University, Université de Sherbrooke, Simon Fraser University, and University of Western Ontario do not offer part-time programs.*

# RATIO OF APPLICATIONS TO ACCEPTANCES
## FOR CO-OP MBA PROGRAMS

*University / Number of applications to acceptance / Ratio of applications to acceptances*

| | | |
|---|---|---|
| McMaster University | 146 : 53 | 2.8 : 1 |
| Université de Sherbrooke | 150 : 40 | 3.8 : 1 |
| University of Windsor | 250 : 24 | 10.4 : 1 |

# Unique Characteristics

- The first year of the University of Alberta's MBA program has nine-tenths of their courses in common with the first year of the Master of Public Management program.

- The University of Calgary has a very strong project orientation resulting in strong contacts with the business community. Its concentration in entrepreneurship and new ventures is very strong.

- Laurentian University/Université Laurentienne is targeting only the part-time market. They do not have a full-time MBA.

- The dean of the University of Manitoba's School of Business comes from the private sector. Most deans, even of business schools, come from the academic side.

- The University of Ottawa/Université d'Ottawa has a new one-year MBA International Stream. Both Ottawa and York University's International programs are only accepting their first official classes in September of 1991, but Ottawa's program seems to be more differentiated from the mainstream MBA than York's. The curriculum at Ottawa is completely separate from the mainstream MBA; whereas at York students in the International MBA share common international courses with students in the mainstream MBA.

- The University of Ottawa/Université d'Ottawa has the only MBA program in Canada that is offered in both French and English. Proficiency in the other language is not required.

- Université de Sherbrooke, McMaster University, and University of Windsor offer the only Co-op MBA programs in Canada.

- The University of Toronto has a compulsory orientation prior to the start of classes. The University of Toronto also has a fast-track part-time program where students complete the MBA in three-and-a-third years and progress through the program in groups so that a sense of camaraderie is established. University of Toronto's MBA program was not a strong contender in the past, but it is certainly one of the more pro-active schools now.

- The University of Western Ontario and Ecoles des Hautes Etudes Commerciales are the only MBA programs in Canada that use the case method almost exclusively.

- Wilfrid Laurier University has a one-year MBA targeted towards candidates with engineering and science degrees.

- York University offers a separate International MBA which requires proficiency in a second language and a work-term abroad.

- York University has the largest MBA enrolment in Canada at 280 students, and Memorial University of Newfoundland has the smallest MBA enrolment at fifteen students.

- Centres for International Business Studies have been established at University of British Columbia, Dalhousie University, Ecoles des Hautes Etudes Commerciales, University of Manitoba, and University of Western Ontario.

- The province of Quebec offers the lowest tuition rates in Canada.


## ONE-YEAR PROGRAMS

- Wilfrid Laurier University
- University of Ottawa/Université d'Ottawa's International Stream MBA
- Université du Québec à Montréal's Executive MBA


## MBA PROGRAMS THAT MAY CONSIDER APPLICANTS WITHOUT UNDERGRADUATE DEGREES

- University of Calgary
- Dalhousie University
- Ecoles des Hautes Etudes Commerciales
- Laurentian University/Université Laurentienne
- Université Laval
- University of Manitoba
- McMaster University
- Memorial University of Newfoundland
- University of Ottawa/Université d'Ottawa
- Université du Québec à Montréal
- Saint Mary's University
- University of Saskatchewan
- Université de Sherbrooke
- University of Western Ontario
- Wilfrid Laurier University
- York University

All the above universities would require applicants without undergraduate degrees to have either a professional designation, e.g., CA, CMA, and/or middle- or upper-management related experience, and/or a high GMAT score, and/or undergraduate courses.

## NO ADVANCED STANDING OFFERED

* Concordia University
* Université Laval
* Université de Sherbrooke
* University of Western Ontario

## UNIVERSITIES THAT DO NOT USE GMAT RESULTS

* Ecoles des Hautes Etudes Commerciales
* Université Laval
* Université de Moncton
* University of Ottawa/Université d'Ottawa (optional)
* Université du Québec à Montréal (only required to clarify marginal cases)
* Université de Sherbrooke

## RECENT WINNERS IN CASE COMPETITIONS

### CONCORDIA CASE COMPETITION

| 1991 | First Place: | Memorial University of Newfoundland |
| | Second Place: | University of Saskatchewan |
| | Third Place: | University of Toronto |
| 1990 | First Place: | Memorial University of Newfoundland |
| | Second Place: | Université Laval |
| | Third Place: | University of New Brunswick |
| 1989 | First Place: | University of Windsor |
| | Second Place: | Memorial University of Newfoundland |
| | Third Place: | Université Laval |

## TECHNOLOGY MANAGEMENT
## CASE COMPETITION

*(This competition started in 1990)*

1991 First Place:        Tie between University of Ottawa/
                         Université d'Ottawa and Ecoles des Hautes
                         Etudes Commerciales
     Second Place:       University of Saskatchewan
     Third Place:        Memorial University of Newfoundland

1990 First Place:        Ecoles des Hautes Etudes Commerciales


## ROYAL BANK PAPER WRITING COMPETITION

1991 First Place:        Dalhousie University
     Second Place:       Dalhousie University
     Third Place:        University of Western Ontario

1990 First Place:        Memorial University of Newfoundland
     Second Place:       University of Western Ontario
     Third Place:        Université Laval

1989 First Place:        University of Western Ontario
     Second Place:       University of Western Ontario
     Third Place:        York University

# Graduate Management Admission Test

The Graduate Management Admission Test is required for admission into most graduate-level business programs in Canada and the United States. For a list of Canadian MBA programs that do not require the GMAT please consult the chapter on "Unique Characteristics." The GMAT is designed to help graduate schools of business assess the qualifications of applicants for advanced study in business and management. The test evaluates each applicant's verbal and mathematical skills. The GMAT consists of three verbal sections, three math sections, and one non-scored trial section. The GMAT does not test specific knowledge obtained in university course work nor does it measure achievement in any particular subject area. Candidates report to the test centre no later than 8:30 a.m. at which the session will close. The examinees are dismissed at approximately 1:00 p.m.

## GENERAL INQUIRIES

Graduate Management Admission Test
Education Testing Service (ETS)
PO Box 6103
Princeton, New Jersey
USA 08541-6103
(609) 771-7330

The following dates and deadlines are correct as of September 1991. Please consult the above address for up-to-date information.

| TEST DATES | DATES FINAL REGISTRATION | SPECIAL REQUESTS RECEIPT DATES |
|---|---|---|
| 19 October 1991 | 23 August 1991 | 6 September 1991 |
| 18 January 1992 | 22 November 1991 | 6 December 1991 |
| 21 March 1992 | 24 January 1992 | 7 February 1992 |
| 28 June 1992 | 24 April 1992 | 8 May 1992 |

A special note concerning registration dates: In 1991 the registration deadline dates have been changed to reflect *the receipt* of the registration. In the past, the registration deadline was for the postmark date. Extensions of the above dates will not be granted under any circumstances. For candidates registering to take the test in Canada, the basic registration fee is $49 in US funds. This fee includes five score reports that are mailed to graduate schools of management. It can take between five to six weeks for test scores to be reported to the schools. Therefore it is advisable to take the GMAT as early as possible to meet schools' application deadline dates.

## TO PREPARE

- The GMAT Bulletin of Information, which contains the registration form for the test, also includes the complete set of instructions for each type of question that may be in the test and a series of sample questions for each type. The GMAT Bulletin of Information is free of charge and is available at universities and through the ETS.

- *The Official Guide for GMAT Review*, prepared by the authors of the test, includes a comprehensive math-review chapter, more than seven hundred test questions with answers and explanations, and test-taking strategies. The book also contains an authentic, recently administered GMAT test with an answer key and scoring instructions.

- *The Official Software for GMAT Review* presents, in an interactive mode, the same sample questions and authentic test that appear in *The Official Guide for GMAT Review* and, like the *Guide*, includes explanations for more than seven hundred test questions. Users will receive immediate feedback about why answers are right or wrong, as well as test-taking strategies and automatic scoring of the actual test. The software package is available for use on an IBM PC or personal System/2 microcomputer and comes complete with a user's manual and a copy of *The Official Guide for GMAT Review*. Both the *Guide* and *The Official Software for GMAT Review* are available through the Graduate Management Admission Test, Educational Testing Service, PO Box 6108, Princeton, NJ USA 08541-6108.

- Preparation courses are also offered by universities and private organizations as well.

# *Appendix*

## ADDRESSES OF CANADIAN MBA SCHOOLS

Associate Dean
MBA Program
Faculty of Business
**UNIVERSITY OF ALBERTA**
Edmonton, Alberta
T6G 2R6
(403) 492-3946

MBA Program
Faculty of Commerce and Business Administration
**UNIVERSITY OF BRITISH COLUMBIA**
2053 Main Mall
Vancouver, British Columbia
V6T 1Y8
(604) 822-8422

The Admissions Committee
MBA Program
Faculty of Management
**UNIVERSITY OF CALGARY**
2500 University Drive North West
Calgary, Alberta
T2N 1N4
(403) 220-3808

The Director
MBA Program
**CONCORDIA UNIVERSITY**
1455 boulevard de Maisonneuve Ouest
Suite GM 201-09
Montréal, Québec
H3G 1M8
(514) 848-2717

School of Business Administration
**DALHOUSIE UNIVERSITY**
6152 Coburg Road
Halifax, Nova Scotia
B3H 1Z5
(902) 494-7080


Bureau du régistraire
**ECOLE DES HAUTES ETUDES COMMERCIALES**
Université de Montréal
5255 avenue Decelles
Montréal, Québec
H3T 1V6
(514) 340-6136


Office of Admissions
**LAURENTIAN UNIVERSITY/UNIVERSITÉ LAURENTIENNE**
Ramsey Lake Road
Sudbury, Ontario
P3C 2C6
(705) 675-1151 extension 3915


Directeur des programmes MBA et DA
Pavilion des sciences de l'administration
**UNIVERSITÉ LAVAL**
Ste-Foy, Québec
G1K 7P4
(418) 656-3521


MBA Program
Faculty of Management
**UNIVERSITY OF MANITOBA**
Winnipeg, Manitoba
R3T 2N2
(204) 474-8448

The McGill MBA Program
Faculty of Management
Samuel Bronfman Building
**MCGILL UNIVERSITY**
1001 rue Sherbrooke Ouest
Montréal, Québec
H3A 1G5
(514) 398-4066

Administrator
MBA Program
Faculty of Business
Kenneth Taylor Hall
Room 118
**MCMASTER UNIVERSITY**
Hamilton, Ontario
L8S 4M4
(416) 525-9140 extension 4433

MBA Program
Faculty of Business Administration
**MEMORIAL UNIVERSITY OF NEWFOUNDLAND**
St. John's, Newfoundland
A1B 3X5
(709) 737-8853

Doyen
Faculté d'administration
**UNIVERSITÉ DE MONCTON**
Moncton, New Brunswick
E1A 3E9
(506) 858-4205

MBA Program
Faculty of Administration
**UNIVERSITY OF NEW BRUNSWICK**
Fredericton, New Brunswick
E3B 5A3
(506) 453-4869

Graduate Programmes
Faculty of Administration
**UNIVERSITY OF OTTAWA/UNIVERSITÉ D'OTTAWA**
136 Jean-Jacques Lussier
Ottawa, Ontario
KIN 6N5
(613) 564-7004


Executive MBA Program/MBA Research
**UNIVERSITÉ DU QUÉBEC À MONTRÉAL**
Boîte Postale 8888, Station A
Montréal, Québec
H3C 3P8
Executive: (514) 987-7704
Research: (514) 987-4448


Assistant Chairman
MBA Program
School of Business
**QUEEN'S UNIVERSITY**
Kingston, Ontario
K7L 3N6
(613) 545-2302


Director of Admissions
MBA Program
**SAINT MARY'S UNIVERSITY**
Halifax, Nova Scotia
B3H 3C3
(902) 420-5414


Assistant Dean (Programs)
College of Commerce
**UNIVERSITY OF SASKATCHEWAN**
Saskatoon, Saskatchewan
S7N 0W0
(306) 966-4785

Programme MBA
Faculté d'administration
**UNIVERSITÉ DE SHERBROOKE**
2500 boulevard Université
Sherbrooke, Québec
J1K 2R1
(819) 821-7333


The Director
MBA Program
Faculty of Business Administration
**SIMON FRASER UNIVERSITY**
Burnaby, British Columbia
V5A 1S6
(604) 291-3639


Faculty of Management Studies
**UNIVERSITY OF TORONTO**
246 Bloor Street West
Toronto, Ontario
M5S 1V4
(416) 978-3499


Student Services — Admissions
Western Business School
Room 116
**UNIVERSITY OF WESTERN ONTARIO**
London, Ontario
N6A 3K7
(519) 661-3212


MBA Program Director
**WILFRID LAURIER UNIVERSITY**
75 University Avenue West
Waterloo, Ontario
N2L 3C5
(519) 884-1970 extension 2544

Faculty of Business Administration
**UNIVERSITY OF WINDSOR**
401 Sunset Avenue
Windsor, Ontario
N9B 3P4
(519) 253-4232


Student Affairs Office
Faculty of Administrative Studies
**YORK UNIVERSITY**
4700 Keele Street
North York, Ontario
M3J 1P3
(416) 736-5060

# CHART 1. AREAS OF CONCENTRATION
# MBA SCHOOLS IN CANADA

Legend:

* Informal concentrations
†† Sub-set concentrations in international business are International Business Finance and Marketing
† Only offered through Co-op or Part-time

| | York University | University of Windsor | Wilfrid Laurier University | University of Western Ontario | University of Toronto | Simon Fraser University | Université de Sherbrooke | University of Saskatchewan | Saint Mary's University | Queen's University | University of Ottawa/Université d'Ottawa | Université de Québec à Montréal (MBA Research) | University of New Brunswick | Université de Moncton | Memorial University | McGill University | McMaster University | University of Manitoba | Université Laval | Laurentian University/Université Laurentienne | Ecole des Hautes Etudes Commerciales | Dalhousie University | Concordia University | University of British Columbia | University of Calgary | University of Alberta |
|---|---|---|---|---|---|---|---|---|---|---|---|---|---|---|---|---|---|---|---|---|---|---|---|---|---|---|
| Accounting | ● | ●* | | | | | ● | | | | | | | | ● | ● | ● | ● | | | ● | | ● | | | |
| Accounting and Finance | ● | | | | | | | | | | | | | | | | | ● | | | | | | | | |
| Accounting and Information Systems | | | | | | | | | | | | | | | | | | | | | | | | | | ● |
| Administrative Studies | | | ●* | | | | | | | | | | | | | | | | | | | | | | | |
| Agribusiness | | | | | | | | | | | | | | | | ● | | | | | | | | | | |
| Arts Administration | ● | | | | | | | | | | | | | | | | | | | | | | | ● | | |
| Business Policy | | | ●* | | | | | | | | | | | | | | | | | | | | | | | |
| Business Statistics | | | | | | | | | | | | | | | | | | | | | | | | ● | | |
| Entrepreneurial Studies | ● | | | | ●* | | | | | | | | | | ● | | | | ● | | | | ● | ● | | |
| Finance | ● | ●* | | ● | | | | | | ● | ● | ●* | | | ● | ● | ● | ● | ●* | ● | ● | | ● | | | |
| General | | | | | | | | | | | | | | | | ● | ● | | | | | | | | | |
| Health Services | | | | | | | | | | | | | | | | | ● | | | | | | | | | |
| Human Resources | | | | | ● | | | | | ● | ● | ●* | | | ● | ● | | | ●* | ● | | | ● | | | |
| Industrial Relations | | | | | | | | | | | ●* | | | | ● | | | | | | | | ● | | | |
| International Business | ● | . | | ●* | | | | ● | ● | ●* | | ††● | ● | | ● | ● | | ● | | | ● | ● | | | | |
| Management Logistics, Production, Operations | | | | | | | | | | | | | | | | ● | | | | | | | | | | |
| Management of Financial Resources | | | | | | | | | | | | | | | | | | | | | | | | | | ● |
| Management of Information Systems | ● | | | | ● | | | | ● | ● | | | | | ● | ● | | ● | | | ● | ● | | | | |
| Management of Public Institutes | | | | | | | | | | | | | | | | | | | | | | | | | | ● |
| Managerial Economics | ● | | | | | | | | | ● | | | | | ● | | | | | | | | | | | |
| Marketing | ● | ●* | | ● | | | | | | ● | ● | ●* | | | ● | ● | ● | ● | ●* | ● | ● | | ● | ● | | |
| Organizational Behaviour | | | | | ● | | | | | ● | | | | | ● | | | | | | | | ● | | | |
| Operations Management | | | | | | | | ● | | ● | | | | | ● | | | ● | | | ● | | | ● | | |
| Personnel | | | | | | | | | | ● | | | | | | | ● | | | | | | | | | |
| Policy Analysis | | | | | | | ● | | | ● | | | | | | | | | | | | | ● | | | |
| Production | | | | | | | | | | | | | | | | | | | | | | | | ● | | |
| Project Management | | | | | | | | | | ● | | | | | ● | | | | | | | | | | | |
| Public Policy | | | | | | | | | | | | | | | | | ● | | | | | | | | | |
| Quantitative Methods | | | | | | | | | | ●* | | | | | ● | | | | | | | | | | | |
| Real Estate and Land Management | ● | | | | | | | | | | | | | | | | | | | | | | | | | |
| Real Property | | | | | | | | | | ● | | | | | | | | | | | | | | | | |
| Strategy | | | | | | | | | | ● | | | | ● | | | | | | | | | | | | |
| Tourism and Hospitality Management | | | | | | | | | | | | | | | | | | | | | | | | ● | | |
| Transport Management | | | | | | | | | | | ● | | | | | | | | | | | | | | | |
| Transport and Logistics | | | | | | | | | | | | | | | | | | | | | | | | ● | | |
| Urban Land Economics | | | | | | | | | | | | | | | | | | | | | | | | ● | | |
| Management Science | ● | ●* | | ● | | | | | | ● | | | | | | | ● | ● | | | | | | ● | | |

## CHART 2. OTHER RELATED PROGRAMS

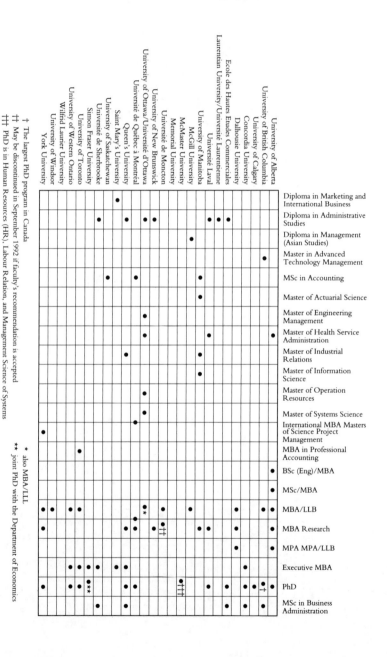

| | University of Alberta | University of British Columbia | University of Calgary | Concordia University | Dalhousie University | Ecole des Hautes Etudes Commerciales | Laurentian University/Université Laurentienne | Université Laval | University of Manitoba | McGill University | McMaster University | Memorial University | Université de Moncton | University of New Brunswick | University of Ottawa/Université d'Ottawa | Université de Québec à Montréal | Queen's University | Saint Mary's University | University of Saskatchewan | Université de Sherbrooke | Simon Fraser University | University of Toronto | University of Western Ontario | Wilfrid Laurier University | University of Windsor | York University |
|---|---|---|---|---|---|---|---|---|---|---|---|---|---|---|---|---|---|---|---|---|---|---|---|---|---|---|
| Diploma in Marketing and International Business | | | | | | | | | | | | | | | | | | • | | | | | | | | |
| Diploma in Administrative Studies | | | | | | • | • | • | | | | | | • | • | | • | | | • | | | | | | |
| Diploma in Management (Asian Studies) | | | | | | | | | | • | | | | | | | | | | | | | | | | |
| Master in Advanced Technology Management | | • | | | | | | | | | | | | | | | | | | | | | | | | |
| MSc in Accounting | | | | | | | | | • | | | | | | | • | | | • | | | | | | | |
| Master of Actuarial Science | | | | | | | | | • | | | | | | | | | | | | | | | | | |
| Master of Engineering Management | | | | | | | | | | | | | | | • | | | | | | | | | | | |
| Master of Health Service Administration | • | | | | | | | • | | | | | | | • | | | | | | | | | | | |
| Master of Industrial Relations | | | | | | | | | • | | | | | | | | • | | | | | | | | | |
| Master of Information Science | | | | | | | | | • | | | | | | | | | | | | | | | | | |
| Master of Operation Resources | | | | | | | | | | | | | | | • | | | | | | | | | | | |
| Master of Systems Science | | | | | | | | | | | | | | | • | | | | | | | | | | | |
| International MBA Masters of Science Project Management | | | | | | | | | | | | | | | | • | | | | | | | | | | • |
| MBA in Professional Accounting | | | | | | | | | | | | | | | | | | | | | | • | | | | |
| BSc (Eng)/MBA | • | | | | | | | | | | | | | | | | | | | | | | | | | |
| MSc/MBA | • | | | | | | | | | | | | | | | | | | | | | | | | | |
| MBA/LLB | • | • | | | • | | | | | • | | | • | | •* | | | | | | | • | • | | • | • |
| MBA Research | • | | | | • | | | • | • | | | | •†† | • | | • | • | | | | | | | | | • |
| MPA MPA/LLB | • | | | | • | | | | | | | | | | | | | | | | | | | | | |
| Executive MBA | | | | • | | | | | | | | | | | | | • | • | | • | • | • | • | | | |
| PhD | • | •† | • | • | | • | | • | | | •††† | | | | | • | • | | | | •** | • | • | | | • |
| MSc in Business Administration | | • | | • | | • | | | | | | | | | | | • | | | • | | | | | | |

† The largest PhD program in Canada

†† May be discontinued in September 1992 if faculty's recommendation is accepted

††† PhD is in Human Resources (HR), Labour Relation, and Management Science of Systems

* also MBA/LLL

** joint PhD with the Department of Economics

## GRAPH 1. PERCENTAGE OF WOMEN IN MBA PROGRAMS IN CANADA IN 1990-91*

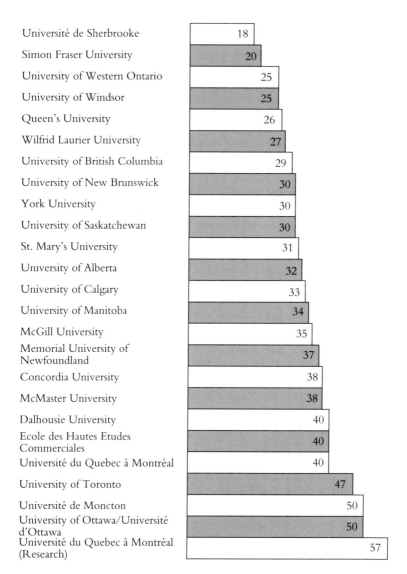

| | |
|---|---|
| Université de Sherbrooke | 18 |
| Simon Fraser University | 20 |
| University of Western Ontario | 25 |
| University of Windsor | 25 |
| Queen's University | 26 |
| Wilfrid Laurier University | 27 |
| University of British Columbia | 29 |
| University of New Brunswick | 30 |
| York University | 30 |
| University of Saskatchewan | 30 |
| St. Mary's University | 31 |
| University of Alberta | 32 |
| University of Calgary | 33 |
| University of Manitoba | 34 |
| McGill University | 35 |
| Memorial University of Newfoundland | 37 |
| Concordia University | 38 |
| McMaster University | 38 |
| Dalhousie University | 40 |
| Ecole des Hautes Etudes Commerciales | 40 |
| Université du Quebec à Montréal | 40 |
| University of Toronto | 47 |
| Université de Moncton | 50 |
| University of Ottawa/Université d'Ottawa | 50 |
| Université du Quebec à Montréal (Research) | 57 |

* Laurentian University/Université Laurentienne's statistics on the percentage of women are not available.

# AVERAGE AGE OF STUDENTS ENTERING MBA PROGRAMS IN CANADA
## (based on the class of 1990)★

Horizontal axis: 24 25 26 27 28 29 30 31 32 33 34 35 36 37

Université de Moncton
University of Windsor
University of Ottawa/Université d'Ottawa
McGill University
McMaster University
Dalhousie University
University of British Columbia
Concordia University
University of Alberta
St. Mary's University
Queen's University
Wilfrid Laurier University
Simon Fraser University
University of Saskatchewan
Memorial University of Newfoundland
University of Western Ontario
York University
University of Manitoba
University of New Brunswick
University of Toronto
Université de Sherbrooke
Ecole des Hautes Etudes Commerciales
University of Calgary
University du Québec à Montréal

★Laurentian University/Université Laurentienne's statistics on the average age of students are not available

**GRAPH 3. OVERVIEW OF AVERAGE AGE OF STUDENTS
ENTERING FULL-TIME MBA PROGRAMS IN CANADA**

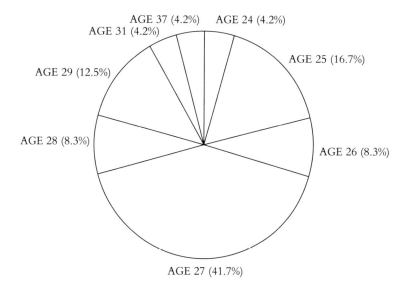

AGE 37 (4.2%)  AGE 24 (4.2%)

AGE 31 (4.2%)

AGE 25 (16.7%)

AGE 29 (12.5%)

AGE 28 (8.3%)

AGE 26 (8.3%)

AGE 27 (41.7%)

## GRAPH 4. RATIO OF APPLICATIONS TO ACCEPTANCES FOR FULL-TIME, PART-TIME, MBA AND CO-OP PROGRAMS IN CANADA FOR 1990-91*

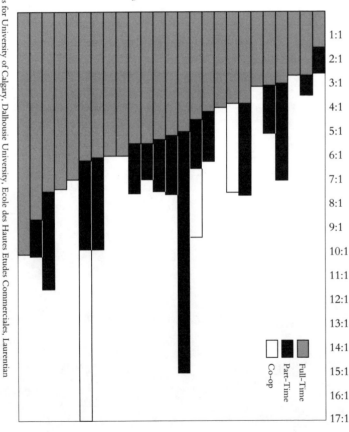

Université de Moncton
University of New Brunswick
University du Québec à Montréal
Wilfrid Laurier University
University of Saskatchewan
Université Laval
St. Mary's University
Université de Sherbrooke
University of Western Ontario
York University
McMaster University
University of Toronto
University of Manitoba
University of British Columbia
Memorial University of Newfoundland
University of Ottawa/Université d'Ottawa
Dalhousie University
Simon Fraser University
Concordia University
University of Windsor
University of Calgary
Queen's University
McGill University
University of Alberta
Ecole des Hautes Etudes Commerciales

1:1
2:1
3:1
4:1
5:1
6:1
7:1
8:1
9:1
10:1
11:1
12:1
13:1
14:1
15:1
16:1
17:1

Co-op  Part-Time  Full-Time

* Data not available for part-time programs for University of Calgary, Dalhousie University, Ecole des Hautes Etudes Commerciales, Laurentian University/Université Laurentienne, Laval Université, or Université de Québec à Montréal. Queen's University, Université de Shetbrooke, Simon Fraser University, and University of Western Ontario do not offer part-time programs.

## LOCATION OF UNIVERSITIES THAT OFFER AN MBA

## Legend For Map of Canada

1. University of Alberta
2. University of British Columbia
3. University of Calgary
4. Concordia University
5. Dalhousie University
6. Ecole des Hautes Etudes Commerciales
7. Laurentian University/Université Laurentienne
8. Université Laval
9. McGill University
10. McMaster University
11. University of Manitoba
12. Memorial University of Newfoundland
13. Université de Moncton

14. University of New Brunswick at Fredericton
15. University of Ottawa/Université d'Ottawa
16. Université du Québec à Montréal
17. Queen's University
18. Saint Mary's University
19. University of Saskatchewan
20. Université de Sherbrooke
21. Simon Fraser University
22. University of Toronto
23. University of Western Ontario
24. Wilfrid Laurier University
25. University of Windsor
26. York University